BILLERICAY

4/7/09

D0716899

&Works.
quality of life

22 AUG 2017

Please return this book on or before the date shown above. To
renew go to www.essex.gov.uk/libraries, ring 0845 603 7628 or
go to any Essex library.

Essex County Council

30130 162220890

First published 2003
Researched and written by Jon Sparks
Field checked and updated 2008 by Andrew McCloy
Series Management: Bookwork Creative Associates
Series Editors: Sandy Draper and Marilynne Lanng
Design and Series Concept: Elizabeth Baldin and Andrew Milne
Picture Research: Vivien Little
Proofreader: Pamela Stagg
Cartography provided by the Mapping Services Department of AA Publishing

Produced by AA Publishing
© Automobile Association Developments Limited 2009

Published by AA Publishing (a trading name of Automobile Association Developments Limited,
whose registered office is Fanum House, Basing View, Basingstoke, Hampshire RG21 4EA;
registered number 1878835)

Enabled by | Ordnance Survey   This product includes mapping data licensed from the Ordnance
Survey® with the permission of the Controller of Her Majesty's
Stationery Office. © Crown Copyright 2009. All rights reserved. Licence number 100021153.

A03627

ISBN: 978-0-7495-6056-0

A CIP catalogue record for this book is available from the British Library.

The contents of this book are believed correct at the time of printing. Nevertheless, the
publishers cannot be held responsible for any errors or omissions or for changes in the
details given in this book or for the consequences of any reliance on the information it
provides. This does not affect your statutory rights. We have tried to ensure accuracy in this
book, but things do change and we would be grateful if readers would advise us of any
inaccuracies they may encounter.

We have taken all reasonable steps to ensure that these walks are safe and achievable by
walkers with a realistic level of fitness. However, all outdoor activities involve a degree of risk
and the publishers accept no responsibility for any injuries caused to readers whilst following
these walks. For more advice on walking safely see page 144. The mileage range shown on the
front cover is for guidance only – some walks may be less than or exceed these distances.

Visit AA Publishing's website www.aatravelshop.com
Colour reproduction by Keenes Group, Andover
Printed by Printer Trento Srl, Italy

Acknowledgements
The Automobile Association would like to thank the following photographers, companies and
picture libraries for their assistance in the preparation of this book.

Abbreviations for the picture credits are as follows: (AA) AA World Travel Library.

3 AA/J Beazley; 9 AA/J Beazley; 16/17 AA/T Marsh; 36/37 AA/J Welsh; 48/49 AA/T Marsh; 70/71
AA/C Jones; 84/85 AA/T Marsh; 107 AA/J Beazley; 110 AA/J Beazley; 124/125 AA/T Marsh

Every effort has been made to trace the copyright holders, and we apologise in advance for
any accidental errors. We would be happy to apply the corrections in the following edition of
this publication.

Right: River Hodder, Forest of Bowland (Walk 36)

AA

50 WALKS IN

Lancashire & Cheshire

50 WALKS OF 2–10 MILES

Contents

WALK		RATING	DISTANCE	PAGE
1	MOW COP	+++	5.25 miles (8.4km)	10
2	LITTLE BUDWORTH	+++	3.5 miles (5.7km)	13
3	BURWARDSLEY	+++	5.5 miles (8.8km)	18
4	PECKFORTON ESTATE	+++	8.5 miles (13.7km)	21
5	CHESTER	+++	2.75 miles (4.4km)	22
6	THURSTASTON	+++	5.25 miles (8.4km)	24
7	THE CLOUD	+++	7 miles (11.3km)	27
8	FRODSHAM HILL	+++	3 miles (4.8km)	30
9	HELSBY HILL	+++	6 miles (9.7km)	33
10	NORTHWICH	+++	5.5 miles (8.8km)	34
11	ALDERLEY EDGE	+++	3.25 miles (5.3km)	38
12	SHUTLINGSLOE	+++	5 miles (8km)	41
13	TEGG'S NOSE	+++	5 miles (8km)	44
14	WHITE NANCY	+++	8.5 miles (13.7km)	47
15	LIVERPOOL	+++	3.75 miles (6km)	48
16	LYME PARK	+++	6.25 miles (10.1km)	50
17	DOVE STONES	+++	8 miles (12.9km)	53
18	DOUGLAS VALLEY	+++	4 miles (6.4km)	58
19	HARROCK HILL	+++	3.75 miles (6km)	61
20	WIGAN PIER	+++	6.25 miles (10.1km)	62
21	FORMBY POINT	+++	3.5 miles (5.7km)	64
22	MARTIN MERE	+++	5 miles (8km)	67
23	HEALEY DELL	+++	2.5 miles (4km)	72
24	ROOLEY MOOR	+++	5.5 miles (8.8km)	75
25	ENTWISTLE	+++	4.25 miles (6.8km)	76
26	BLACKSTONE EDGE	+++	6.5 miles (10.4km)	78
27	ANGLEZARKE	+++	7.25 miles (11.7km)	81
28	HASLINGDEN GRANE	+++	3.5 miles (5.7km)	86
29	HOG LOW PIKE	+++	6.75 miles (10.9km)	89
30	LEVER PARK	+++	3.75 miles (6km)	90

Contents

WALK		RATING	DISTANCE	PAGE
31	DARWEN TOWER	+++	4 miles (6.4km)	92
32	WYCOLLER	+++	5.25 miles (8.4km)	95
33	PENDLE HILL	+++	4.75 miles (7.7km)	98
34	PENDLE HILL	+++	6 miles (9.7km)	101
35	WITTON COUNTRY PARK	+++	4.5 miles (7.2km)	102
36	HODDER VALLEY	+++	7 miles (11.3km)	104
37	DUNSOP BRIDGE	+++	9.25 miles (14.9km)	108
38	HURST GREEN	+++	6.5miles (10.4km)	112
39	BIRDY BROW	+++	8 miles (12.9km)	115
40	CLITHEROE	+++	3.5 miles (5.7km)	116
41	KNOTT END	+++	5.5 miles (8.8km)	118
42	BEACON FELL	+++	6 miles (9.7km)	121
43	CROOK O'LUNE	+++	3.25 miles (5.3km)	126
44	CROOK O'LUNE	+++	8.25 miles (13.3km)	129
45	GLASSON	+++	5.5 miles (8.8km)	130
46	CLOUGHA PIKE	+++	5.25 miles (8.4km)	132
47	LECK BECK	+++	7.5 miles (12.1km)	135
48	SILVERDALE	+++	5.5 miles (8.8km)	138
49	SILVERDALE	+++	8.75 miles (14.1km)	141
50	LANCASTER	+++	3 miles (4.8km)	142

Rating

Each walk is rated for its relative difficulty compared to the other walks in this book. Walks marked +++ are likely to be shorter and easier with little total ascent. The hardest walks are marked +++

Walking in Safety

For advice and safety tips see page 144.

Locator Map

Legend

--→--	Walk Route		▦	Built-up Area
❶	Route Waypoint		▦	Woodland Area
– – –	Adjoining Path		🚻	Toilet
☀	Viewpoint		🅿	Car Park
•	Place of Interest		⊞	Picnic Area
⌂	Steep Section		)(	Bridge

Introducing Lancashire and Cheshire

In 1974 we were told that the 'new' counties were purely administrative and wouldn't sweep away historical identities. It doesn't seem to have worked that way. It's hard to remember that, only a generation ago, Liverpool and Manchester were both in Lancashire, as was a good chunk of the Lake District. Boundaries change, and so do landscapes. The landscapes of this region bear the imprint of millennia of human activity. Chester was a great Roman centre, but Lancashire something of a backwater. Until a century after the Norman Conquest it was ruled partly from Cheshire and partly from Yorkshire. It gained wealth and importance slowly through the following centuries.

A rich history

From the middle of the 18th century, accelerating change reshaped the face of the region and made it the centre of developments that rippled out across the entire world. Within the span of a single human life canals, railways and steam-powered factories all made their first appearance. The world's first commercial railway, between Liverpool and Manchester, opened in 1830. Only 14 years later regular trains were running between London and Lancaster. During the Industrial Revolution, the region had a significance at least as great as Silicon Valley today.

Yet, only a few miles from these hotbeds of change, large areas remained sparsely populated and seemingly untouched. Most of Cheshire, and most of present-day Lancashire, is open country, from the high moors to the pastures and arable fields. The classic English landscape of hedges, woods and fields survives better in Cheshire and Lancashire than in many other shires. However, we shouldn't imagine that this landscape is 'timeless'. It's a creation of an agricultural revolution that ran parallel with industrial change.

That these changes happened at the same time is no coincidence. Agricultural developments made the industrial ones possible. Areas like the Cheshire Plain and West Lancashire played a vital role in feeding the expanding towns. Potatoes, imported from the New World, were soon a staple. Fish (from Fleetwood) and chips (from Pilling or Ormskirk potatoes) is another tradition that began around this time.

PUBLIC TRANSPORT

The region is well covered by public transport. Nearly all the walks can be reached using either buses or trains, and it's especially appropriate for the more urban walks. Sometimes it will be logical to start the walk at a different point on the circuit. There is comprehensive telephone information on 0870 6082608, while National Rail Enquiries are on 08457 48 49 50 or online (www.totaljourney.com).

Industrial heritage

If these areas fed the workers, then Lancaster and Liverpool fed the mills with imported cotton. Stone was quarried from the hills and coal from under the fields. The story of the region is one of change, but change is not a one-way street. There are new towns growing like topsy, and empty valleys where hundreds or thousands once lived. Areas which were once intensively farmed are now empty moorland. Old quarries are colonised by rock climbers, and by peregrine falcons. Of the numerous railway lines that closed in the 1960s, many are now invaluable for walkers and cyclists. Canals have traded commerce for pleasure-boating, angling, wildlife and of course for walking. These layers of history add fascination to most of the walks. You can delve into industrial archaeology or see how 'abandoned' sites often provide a richer habitat for wildlife than modern farming allows.

Still, when you really want to get away from it all, there are always places touched by wildness; dragonfly-haunted wetlands, ancient woodlands, hidden valleys and rocky ridges. Above all, there are the vast moors. An old music chimes in the names of beck and fell, and there's music older still in the curlew's bubbling cry, drifting across skylines that haven't changed since the ice age.

Using this book

INFORMATION PANELS

An information panel for each walk shows its relative difficulty (see page 5), the distance and total amount of ascent. An indication of the gradients you will encounter is shown by the rating ▲ ▲ ▲ (no steep slopes) to ▲ ▲ ▲ (several very steep slopes).

MAPS

There are 30 maps, covering 40 of the walks. Some walks have a suggested option in the same area. The information panel for these walks will tell you how much extra walking is involved. On short-cut suggestions the panel will tell you the total distance if you set out from the start of the main walk. Where an option returns to the same point on the main walk, just the distance of the loop is given. Where an option leaves the main walk at one point and returns to it at another, then the distance shown is for the whole walk. The minimum time suggested is for reasonably fit walkers and doesn't allow for stops. Each walk has a suggested map.

START POINTS

The start of each walk is given as a six-figure grid reference prefixed by two letters indicating which 100km square of the National Grid it refers to. You'll find more information on grid references on most Ordnance Survey maps.

DOGS

We have tried to give dog owners useful advice about how dog friendly each walk is. Please respect other countryside users. Keep your dog under control, especially around livestock, and obey local bylaws and other dog control notices.

CAR PARKING

Many of the car parks suggested are public, but occasionally you may find you have to park on the roadside or in a lay-by. Please be considerate when you leave your car, ensuring that access roads or gates are not blocked and that other vehicles can pass safely.

Right: Alderley Edge, Cheshire Plain (Walk 11)

Down and Up Again to Mow Cop

A walk that samples both the lush Cheshire Plain and the wilder ridges that overlook it.

DISTANCE 5.25 miles (8.4km)   **MINIMUM TIME** 2hrs 15min

ASCENT/GRADIENT 720ft (219m) ▲▲▲   **LEVEL OF DIFFICULTY** ✦✦✦

PATHS Open fields and woodland paths, canal tow path, quiet lanes, short sections where path indistinct, 10 stiles

LANDSCAPE Mostly farmland and deciduous woods on flanks of ridge, views from crest

SUGGESTED MAP OS Explorer 268 Wilmslow, Macclesfield & Congleton

START / FINISH Grid reference: SJ 857573

DOG FRIENDLINESS Woods and canal tow path are best places to let dogs run

PARKING National Trust car park directly below Mow Cop castle

PUBLIC TOILETS In nearby towns of Kidsgrove or Biddulph

Some people might think it odd to start a walk on the top of a hill, descend, and then climb up again, but then Mow Cop is an odd place. Its crooked streets seem positively to seek the steepest ways. Split between the two counties of Cheshire and Staffordshire, the village is as quirky as the castle that dominates it. Never a fortress, the castle was built principally for embellishment and remains one of England's best-known and most conspicuous follies.

View From a Hill

It's not the view to it that concerns us, however, so much as the view from. Mow Cop is perched on a sharp ridge, the last great outlier of the millstone grit. The view south is over the Potteries but north and west is the green expanse of the Cheshire Plain. The distinct boundary between hill and plain is underlined by the Macclesfield Canal.

The walk starts level, passing the Old Man of Mow. Logic suggests that this monolith is merely an incidental remnant left behind when the quarries closed. Yet it's so sculpted that you can't help feeling that, consciously or not, there was some artistry at work here. This is a good place to pause and study the view before descending to the plain.

The descent is steepest in the woods of Roe Park. Down on the level, you first cross the main Manchester to Stoke-on-Trent high-speed railway line via a new underpass. Just beyond, and on a parallel course, is the peaceful Macclesfield Canal, where the speed limit is a sedate 4mph (6.4kph). Though the general line of the canal was planned by Thomas Telford, the principal engineer was William Crossley.

The Path Vanishes

On the way up again, you need to be alert for a short section in the woods past Limekiln Farm. The path tries to hide in the undergrowth, then doubles back sharply as if trying to shake off pursuit. Higher up, there is a section with no clear path at all, but it is simply a matter of following the edge of a field.

Overall the ascent is less steep than the descent, but there's rough ground below the ridge crest. Here, if you so desire, you can walk with one foot in Cheshire and the other in Staffordshire. A path then threads a narrow belt of woodland before emerging into another old quarry. No Old Men here, but in summer the level floor is alive with wild flowers.

WALK 1 DIRECTIONS

❶ Head towards the castle. Before reaching it take a narrower path left, to a road. Go right up this, then left, signposted 'Gritstone Trail' and 'South Cheshire Way'. Swing left, then right, then fork right on a narrow path past the Old Man. Rejoin the wider track, heading towards a communications mast.

❷ At a junction of footpaths go left. Follow the field-edges downhill and continue descending in a wood. Where the footpath splits at a huge tangle of holly

WALK

1

bushes go left and into a field, then bear right. Skirt a farm then join a rough track. Keep heading downhill to join a surfaced lane. Bear left and cross beneath the railway at Ackers Crossing.

❸ Follow the lane to a wider road and turn right. Cross over a canal bridge, then go down steps and left, along the tow path. At bridge No 81 go up to a lane and turn left, over the bridge.

❹ Follow the narrow lane to reach a crossroads by Baytree Farm and go straight ahead up the track to Limekiln Farm. Take a track on the left just beyond the buildings. Keep low, along the edge of the wood, until the track bends right by a post marked with yellow arrows.

❺ Go left, pushing through undergrowth to duckboards and a stile. Turn right along a field edge. After 100yds (91m) there's another post. Descend sharp right then cross several, sometimes

slippery, plank bridges. A narrow path heads uphill leading to a wider track, then tarmac near a house. Before the track starts to descend again, go right to a stile. Follow the left edge of a field alongside a wood. After another stile go up a narrower field until it opens out. Above a signpost, go right on a green track to a stile amid holly trees. Continue to another boundary; beyond is rougher ground with rushes and some gorse and a firm track curves across this to reach a stile on the far side. Bear left up a drive to the road, then follow it right for 300yds (274m).

❻ By a gateway on the right-hand side a Gritstone Trail sign lurks under a beech tree, pointing the way into a narrow wood. The footpath roughly follows the upper margin of the wood, then emerges on the level floor of some old quarry workings. Bear left up steps, below the communications tower, to rejoin the outward route near the Old Man of Mow.

Woods and Heaths of Little Budworth

An easy walk centred around the distinctive heathland of Little Budworth Country Park.

WALK 2

DISTANCE 3.5 miles (5.7km)	**MINIMUM TIME** 1hr 15min
ASCENT/GRADIENT 98ft (30m) ▲▲▲	**LEVEL OF DIFFICULTY** +++
PATHS Easy tracks at first, field paths and some (usually quiet) road walking, 13 stiles	
LANDSCAPE Mature woodland, open heath, farmland and mere	
SUGGESTED MAP OS Explorer 267 Northwich & Delamere Forest	
START / FINISH Grid reference: SJ 590654	
DOG FRIENDLINESS Can run free in country park and fenced track	
PARKING Main car park for Little Budworth Country Park	
PUBLIC TOILETS At start	

In the middle of all the rich green farmland of lowland Cheshire is an island of something different, a little piece of a rougher, older landscape. As ever, though, to call it 'wild' would be misleading. There is probably no such thing as a truly wild landscape anywhere in England. Usually it's peaceful, but a word of warning – it is very close to the Oulton Park motor-racing circuit. On race days not only is the traffic abominable, there's no escaping the noise either.

Lowland Heath

The area now called Little Budworth Country Park is a fragment of lowland heath. Britain has a substantial proportion of the world's lowland heath, but there is a lot less than there used to be – only 18 per cent of what was recorded in 1800. Most of what remains is in Southern England, so all in all, Little Budworth is a bit special.

Open landscape

The essence of heath is an open landscape, with a mix of heather, gorse, bracken and grasses and with only scattered, if any, trees. Gorse is unmistakable and in summer the popping of its seed pods makes it one of those rare plants you can recognise with your ears. There are two characteristic species of heather: ling (which gardeners may know as Calluna vulgaris) and bell heather (Erica cinerea). They often grow together and look quite similar, but ling has slightly paler and more open flowers.

Heathland typically developed from areas cleared of trees from neolithic times onward, as the poor soil made it unsuitable for permanent cultivation. The land was, however, still used for grazing. Gorse was traditionally used as fuel and for animal fodder, while bracken provided animal bedding and was also a valuable source of potash. These activities, and the occasional natural fire, prevented the heath reverting to woodland. Much of today's country park is wooded, but you will also see large areas of heath, including some which have recently been cleared.

13

WALK 2

The Margins of Budworth Mere

The majority of the heathland at Little Budworth is dry, but there are some low-lying wetter areas. The pool you pass on the walk is a breeding ground for dragonflies and damselflies. By contrast the second half of the walk crosses farmland and then skirts the reedy margins of Budworth Mere. Many of Cheshire's meres were created by subsidence resulting from salt mining. Such relatively new lakes are also often called 'flashes'. Others, like this one were formed in hollows in the lumpy mantle of 'drift' left by retreating ice at the end of the last ice age.

Finally the walk visits Little Budworth village. It is peaceful and attractive but not so outrageously pretty that it has become a tourist magnet. You'll probably agree that this is to its benefit.

WALK 2 DIRECTIONS

❶ From the car park walk straight across the Coach Road to a path and then turn right on a wider path. Fork left and follow the main path, keeping straight on at a crossroads and again at the next crossing. When a field appears ahead, follow the path alongside to its right. This veers away right. Go back left just before a cleared area, by a Heathland Trail marker.

LITTLE BUDWORTH

2 Go right on a wide track to the Coach Road and straight across into Beech Road. After 200yds (183m) turn right on a well-used path through open and attractive woodland. Go through a gap in the fence, beyond which the path, curves round a larger pool fringed with reeds and other vegetation — it is a magnet for wildlife.

3 Cross a causeway/dam by the pool and gently climb a sunken track beyond. As it levels out, fork left by a Heathland Trail sign then turn left, with an open field not far away to the left. Bear left on a wider surfaced track, swinging down past houses to an ornamental pool in a dip. Immediately after this turn right on a sandy track.

4 Where another path crosses, most people evidently go through a gate ahead into the corner of the field. Strictly speaking, however, the right of way goes over a stile to its right then across the (very wet and smelly) corner of a wood to a second stile. From here bear right under a power line, to a stile in the far corner. Follow a narrow path (beware nettles), then go over a stile on the right and straight across a large field. Aim just left of the farm to a gate and stile. Go left on a lane for 60yds (55m) then right down a track. This becomes narrower, then descends slightly.

5 As it levels out, there's a stile on the right, with a sign for Budworth Mere. Go down towards the water then left on a path skirting the mere. At the end go right up a road, swinging further right into the centre of Little Budworth.

6 Keep straight ahead along the road, going through the village then past open fields. Approaching the former entrance gates of Oulton Park, the pavement comes to an end. Here take a narrow woodland path on the right back to the car park.

Overleaf: Burwardsley, Cheshire Plain (Walk 3)

Views of Cheshire's Castle Country

A loop walk on the most accessible section of a prominent sandstone ridge.

DISTANCE 5.5 miles (8.8km) **MINIMUM TIME** 2hrs

ASCENT/GRADIENT 919ft (280m) ▲▲▲ **LEVEL OF DIFFICULTY** ✦✦✦

PATHS Field and woodland paths, plus some lane walking; 6 stiles

LANDSCAPE Richly varied woodland and farmland, some rocky outcrops and views over lush plains

SUGGESTED MAP OS Explorer 257 Crewe & Nantwich

START / FINISH Grid reference: SJ 521551

DOG FRIENDLINESS On lead in Peckforton Estate and near grazing stock. Beware of electric fences

PARKING Verges at end of tarmac on Coppermines Lane, off A534 car park and picnic area

PUBLIC TOILETS None en route

Beeston Castle, which is visible from afar, was built in the 13th century, its strategic hilltop site looking towards the turbulent Welsh border. It saw no real battles until the English Civil War around 400 years later. After changing hands several times, it was largely demolished in 1646 on the orders of Parliament. Nearby Peckforton Castle is a 19th-century imitation of a medieval fortress.

Layers of History

Distant views of these grand castle-crowned ridges might lead you to anticipate airy ridge walking. In fact there is little of that to be found here, though Raw Head hill does provide its own brand of unique moments of drama. Generally, however, this walk delivers something different and equally pleasurable for walkers.

The castles proclaim the long history of the area, but there are other layers of history to be found. The name of Coppermines Lane, where the walk starts, is a reminder of an industrial element. Where the walk first leaves the tarmac, a chimney glimpsed below marks the site of the old copper works. Just above, the map still marks the site of a mine, though there's little to be seen of it now.

Sandstone Trail

From here your route climbs to Raw Head hill, then continues along a steep slope which breaks into startling crags at Musket's Hole. The summit, at 745ft (227m), is the highest point on the Sandstone Trail, a 34-mile (55km) route from Frodsham (see Walk 8) to Whitchurch. However, a screen of trees means it is far from the best viewpoint. The walk does serve up some great views, but never an all-round panorama: more a series of tasty morsels than a grand main course. But there is plenty of charm in their sudden and often fleeting appearance.

BURWARDSLEY

High Point

After Raw Head hill the walk winds down through woods, fields and along a quiet lane to Burwardsley village then up an even quieter one to Higher Burwardsley. Then it climbs again to the National Trust-owned Bulkeley Hill Wood. The high point, literally and metaphorically, is a wonderful grove of sweet chestnut trees on a broad shelf rimmed by low sandstone crags. With virtually no undergrowth, you can fully appreciate the gnarled, multi-stemmed trees, which seem hunched with age. From here it is an enjoyable and easy stroll down through a plantation and then across a field back to reach Coppermines Lane.

WALK 3 DIRECTIONS

1 Walk down Coppermines Lane to a sharp left-hand bend. Cross a stile beside an arched sandstone overhang. Cross a field then ascend the edge of a wooded area. Cross fields to the edge of another wood. Go up right, signposted 'Raw Head, Beeston', joining a track towards Chiflik Farm.

2 Go through a kissing gate by the farm and up a fenced path. The path generally runs just below the top of a steep slope, climbing to the trig point on Raw Head hill.

3 The path goes right and into a slight dip. Go left down steps then back right, slanting through a steep plantation. Go left down a narrow lane for 300yds (274m). Opposite a track and footpath sign, descend through newly planted woodland. At the bottom cross a stile and go up towards Bodnook Cottage. Just below this bear left and into a wood. Follow a firm path, roughly level then slightly left and downhill among spindly beech trees.

4 Cross a stile at the edge of the wood, then another immediately to its right. There's a faint path, aim directly for a stile below a large tree, 50yds (46m) left of a house. Continue through the next field. At the far end cross a stile and follow the road ahead.

5 On the edge of Burwardsley village turn right up the first lane. Go right again up Sarra Lane, then fork left at an 'Unsuitable for Motor Vehicles' sign. Follow the lane up past Cheshire Workshops. Just beyond this the road forks.

6 Go right and over the junction up Rock Lane. Keep right at the next fork. The lane meets the Crewe and Nantwich boundary.

> **WHERE TO EAT AND DRINK**
>
> The Pheasant Inn, in Higher Burwardsley, is only a few paces from the route. There's outdoor seating with an excellent view, real ale and good food. After the walk, try The Bickerton Poacher on the A534 near Coppermines Lane.

7 Just before the boundary sign go right through a gate and follow the field-edge path. Keep ahead to meet a narrow lane and go up left. On the crest, opposite a gatehouse, go right on a track into Bulkeley Hill Wood.

8 Go left up steps into the wood and continue less steeply. Where the path splits, the left branch follows the brink of a steep slope. Keep fairly close to this edge as the path levels. Go through a gap in a fence then descend through a plantation, to a kissing gate beside a big iron gate. Go diagonally right on a clear track across a field to Coppermines Lane.

> **WHAT TO LOOK OUT FOR**
>
> Sweet chestnuts, like those in Bulkeley Hill Wood, are not a native species; they probably arrived with the Romans. Nor are they related to the horse chestnut, which gets its name from the chance resemblance of its fruit. In fact the sweet chestnut is related to the oaks.

> **WHILE YOU'RE THERE**
>
> Peckforton Castle isn't open to visitors, but Beeston Castle is – and to the elements too. Much of it is in ruins, apart from the gatehouse and some towers of the outer wall. Its condition seems perfectly fitting for the atmospheric site.

On Peckforton's Estate

More classic Cheshire farmland and richly varied woods.

See map and information panel for Walk 3

DISTANCE *8.5 miles (13.7km)* **MINIMUM TIME** *3hrs*
ASCENT/GRADIENT *1,200ft (366m)* ▲▲▲ **LEVEL OF DIFFICULTY** +++

WALK 4 DIRECTIONS (Walk 3 option)

At the fork (Point **6**) keep left, then go straight across the crossroads into Pennsylvania Lane, passing The Pheasant Inn. Follow the lane for 350yds (320m) to a stile on the left under a large oak tree. Follow the hedge down to a stile in the corner, then slant down to a concealed stile in the bottom corner of the next field.

Turn right down the lane. Just inside the entrance of Outlanes Farm (Point **A**) go right, over stiles skirting the farm, then left behind the large shed. Cross a small footbridge and go up right to the next stile. Bear left to two trees on the rise and then down to a small gap in the hedge, directly in line with the large farm.

At the edge of the farm compound (Point **B**) cross a stile on the right by a gate and double back along the field's right edge. Enjoy the classic view of Beeston Castle on its crag-fringed hilltop.

Cross a small footbridge and go half left up a short slope. Pass right of a dew pond to the next stile, in a broken hedge line. Though quite new, this stile appears redundant – except when there's an electric fence along this boundary!

Keep parallel to the edge of wood to another stile, then bear right to a small footbridge. Just beyond is a signpost. Follow a diagonal line through crops to another fingerpost (Point **C**) and go left along the track. This becomes a lane lined with cottages, many in distinctive Peckforton Estate livery and eminently photogenic.

Just past Oak Cottage, go sharp right on a track to continue gently up through woods. Go over a crossroads of routes. As the track finally starts to descend (Point **D**) fork left on a narrower path, with a Sandstone Trail sign 'Bulkeley Hill'. The path climbs across a very steep slope, decorated with sandstone outcrops and tree roots. At the crest, ignore the gate ahead and go down to the right, through a gate, then follow a path alongside a wall.

Keep straight ahead, to a kissing gate on the bend of a lane, and go left. In 100yds (91m) you reach a T-junction and rejoin Walk 3. Go up left, and the Crewe and Nantwich boundary sign (Point **7**) is 100yds (91m) ahead.

Chester's Walls and Water

The classic circuit of Chester's medieval walls, with a few variations.

DISTANCE 2.75 miles (4.4km)   MINIMUM TIME 1hr

ASCENT/GRADIENT 164ft (50m) ▲▲▲   LEVEL OF DIFFICULTY +++

PATHS *Pavements and surfaced paths*

LANDSCAPE *Historic but crowded urban scene, racecourse and river*

SUGGESTED MAP *OS Explorer 266 Wirral & Chester*

START / FINISH *Grid reference: SJ 407664*

DOG FRIENDLINESS *Unlikely to feel welcome on streets and narrow wall path*

PARKING *Park-and-Ride at Upton and on A548, A483 and A41*

PUBLIC TOILETS *On Frodsham Street and at Chester Visitor Centre*

WALK 5 DIRECTIONS

From Frodsham Street, turn right into Foregate Street then under the clock into Eastgate Street and along to High Cross. Turn right on to Northgate Street. Where it opens out turn left through a gap into Hamilton Place. In 20yds (18m), on the right, a window shows the strongroom of the Roman headquarters or Principia.

Return to Northgate Street and continue to the grand Town Hall of 1869. Turn right under the 14th-century Abbey Gate into Georgian Abbey Square. Overlooking the neat buildings is the cathedral. Its exterior is largely Victorian but much of the older fabric can still be seen

inside. Leave the square by Abbey Street and go up on to the walls. Turn left past the Deanery Field, to the Phoenix or King Charles Tower, where Charles I watched his army's heavy defeat at the Battle of Rowton Moor. Follow the walls round, overlooking the deep cutting of the Shropshire Union Canal. As you reach Northgate Bridge, on the right is the Bluecoat School, founded in 1717 to counter 'the growth of vice and debauchery in Chester.'

Continue to another tower, Morgan's Mount. Descend steps on the left, loop through the arch and descend to canal level. To your right is the cutting, carved in solid sandstone. Go left along the tow path to Northgate Locks. This unusual 'staircase lock' comes with full instructions. The drop is 33ft (10m). Below the locks the canal squeezes under the railway bridge, then the path forks.

Follow the tow path round under another bridge to Northgate Basin. Just across the water is Telford's warehouse, with its arched loading dock. Return to the fork, go up to railings then turn left up steps and back to the walls. Turn right to Bonewaldesthorne's Tower, which guarded the harbour until the river changed its course.

The Water Tower and connecting wall were built in 1332 to protect the port. There's a good view here of the railway. This section of line into North Wales was built in 1846. Lines from an 1856 guidebook, quoted on a wall plaque, suggest how railways were viewed, 'Whew! With a rush like that of a tiger from his den…Full 40 miles an hour.'

Continue down City Walls Road; the top of the wall is level with the road for a stretch. Pass the Queen's School then take the higher level, over Watergate Bridge. Just beyond this there's a good view of Chester Racecourse, said to be Britain's first. The course occupies an area called the Roodee, once a tidal pool, but silted up by medieval times.

Cross busy Grosvenor Road at the traffic-lights to the continuation of the walls below Chester Castle. The medieval castle was replaced by a series of Greek revival buildings in the 1790s. When the walls sink to road level, cross to a path overlooking the river. Cross the Dee Bridge, with its pioneering hydro-electric station from 1913. Turn left along the far

bank, past ugly modern flats and a restored waterwheel, to Queen's Park. Go up steps and recross the river by Queen's Park Bridge. The footbridge was built in 1923 and bounces gently as you walk across.

Climb steps above the end of the bridge and 20yds (18m) further on turn left through a gate to the ruins of St John's Church, Chester's first cathedral. Continue along the side of the 19th-century church and round its west front to emerge alongside the remains of the Roman amphitheatre. It is the largest amphitheatre in Britain, with walls once 35ft (10m) high, though it's hard to imagine how it could hold 7,000 spectators.

Just beyond, on the left, are the Roman Gardens. The gardens date from the 1950s, but do contain a collection of Roman masonry. Go under the arch of Newgate and turn left immediately on Park Street, past a multi-storey car park to the graceful almshouses known as Nine Houses (there used to be more). Go up a ramp on to the walls and go left over Newgate.

Continue along the walls past the glass-cased remains of Thimbleby's Tower and on to the 18th-century Eastgate, surmounted by the elaborate clock erected to mark Queen Victoria's Diamond Jubilee. Just beyond, descend steps on the right to complete the circuit.

Uncommon Delights at Thurstaston

Panoramic views from a heathland crest, and the edge of a grand estuary.

DISTANCE 5.25 miles (8.4km) **MINIMUM TIME** 1hr 45min

ASCENT/GRADIENT 345ft (105m) ▲▲▲ **LEVEL OF DIFFICULTY** +++

PATHS Some road walking, sandy tracks and bare rock, then field paths, 2 stiles

LANDSCAPE Woodland and heath, farmland, seashore

SUGGESTED MAP OS Explorer 266 Wirral & Chester

START / FINISH Grid reference: SJ 238834

DOG FRIENDLINESS Dogs have several opportunities to roam

PARKING Wirral Country Park at bottom of Station Road, Thurstaston

PUBLIC TOILETS In Country Park Visitor Centre adjacent to car park

---

This is a walk of two distinct halves. It is somewhat unfortunate that the busy A540 underlines this division, but not that there is so much variety in a small space. You start near to the shoreline but, saving that for the end, climb long straight Station Road. This is an uninspiring opening but easy and quick so don't let it put you off. The grand Church of St Bartholomew signals the end of the beginning and once the main road is crossed you are on Thurstaston Common.

Thurstaston Common

Many people expect 'common' to be open but the name really refers to common grazing. Where this right is no longer exercised, unless the land is managed in some way, it's quite normal for it to revert to woodland. In fact most of the common is wooded but there are still good open stretches where heathland survives. It's obviously difficult for trees to gain a foothold in the thin sandy soils of the more exposed parts.

Most of the ground is dry but there are a few damper hollows. One such hollow is skirted early on. In summer it's marked by the white tassels of cotton grass. The wet patches are also home to cross-leaved heath, not the ling and bell heather of the drier areas. Its flowers grow in clusters rather than spikes. Also found are sundews, low-growing plants with reddish, hairy, sticky leaves. These trap insects from which the plant gains nutrients lacking in the poor soils.

Just below the summit you break out on to a bare sandstone crest which gives a view over the Dee Estuary and out to sea. On a clear day the Great Orme behind Llandudno stands out boldly, as does an offshore wind farm out in the Irish Sea. From the summit itself the view spreads to include the Liverpool cathedrals. The Forest of Bowland and Winter Hill rise to their left, and you can also identify Formby Point (see Walk 21).

After retracing your steps as far as the church, the second half of this walk begins innocuously across farmland, but as you descend towards the sea, there's an unexpected moment of drama as you arrive at the ravine of the Dungeon, complete with tiny waterfall.

THURSTASTON

Below this you join the old railway which is now the Wirral Way. Past ponds, home to water-lilies and moorhens, you soon reach the brink of the slope about 50ft (15m) above the estuary. It's stretching it a bit to call it a cliff, but it's steep enough to be no place to slip. There's little solid rock exposed in these 'cliffs', which are composed of boulder clay. This is nearly the end of the walk, but you may want to linger and savour the view across the wide estuary to Wales.

WALK 6 DIRECTIONS

❶ From the car park, loop round past the visitor centre and wildlife pond, go out to Station Road

and go straight up for 0.5 mile (800m). At the top it swings right.

❷ Turn left before the church and go up to the A540. Go left,

WALK 6

past the Cottage Loaf, then go right through a kissing gate. Follow the track ahead past a school to the end of a cul-de-sac.

❸ Go through a kissing gate to a broad path then go right on a smaller path. Cross a track near a cattle grid then beyond a wide gate swing left to join another track. This keeps just inside the edge of the wood, following the course of Greasby Brook.

❹ A boundary wall appears ahead. Turn left alongside it. Where it ends keep ahead, passing the model railway. Alongside Royden Park the wall resumes. Where it ends again turn left by a sign and map. Cross a clearing to a junction.

❺ Twenty yards (18m) further on is a kissing gate. Turn right before it, on a narrow path. At a T-junction turn right, then at the end of this go left on a broader path. Beyond a marker stone continue over tree roots and bare rock, then at a junction of paths among light woodland and with a drop ahead go left. Follow the wide and soon open edge of the rocky escarpment up to a sandstone pillar with a map/view indicator and then the trig point. Continue the short distance to the

end of the ridge and take the left fork. Descend a broad path that rejoins the outward route. Retrace your steps past the Cottage Loaf and down the top section of Station Road.

❻ Turn left past the church. When the road swings round to the left, a lane continues straight ahead. Cross a stile and follow a well-marked footpath. In a dip cross a stream and turn right at a footpath sign. After recrossing the stream, zig-zag down a steeper slope into The Dungeon.

❼ Cross the stream again and follow it down. Climb on to an old railway embankment and go right. When green gates bar the way, sidestep left. Continue for another 220yds (201m) to a gap in the hedge. Follow a path, winding past a couple of ponds then out to the cliff tops above the estuary. Go right for 240yds (219m), then bear right across grass towards the visitor centre and the car park.

Viewing The Cloud from Both Sides

WALK 7

An exhilarating walk with a long, easy prelude then a steep ascent to one of Cheshire's best viewpoints.

DISTANCE *7 miles (11.3km)* **MINIMUM TIME** *2hrs 30min*

ASCENT/GRADIENT *804ft (245m)* ▲▲▲ **LEVEL OF DIFFICULTY** +++

PATHS *Field paths, canal tow path, some lanes, rougher and steeper on The Cloud, 5 stiles*

LANDSCAPE *Meadows and fields along canal, craggy summit*

SUGGESTED MAP *OS Explorer 268 Wilmslow, Macclesfield & Congleton*

START / FINISH *Grid reference: SJ 895627*

DOG FRIENDLINESS *Can run free on tow path and upper reaches of The Cloud*

PARKING *Car park by picnic area on Weathercock Lane, Timbersbrook*

PUBLIC TOILETS *At car park*

It's an enticing name, The Cloud, and the views from the crag-fringed crest live up to the promise. Instead of a direct attack this walk first makes a wide, easy sweep around the hill. This is attractive in its own right and gives you a greater feel for the landscape you'll ultimately survey.

Along the Macclesfield Canal

Even so, a downhill start may seem perverse. In fact the height lost is minimal and the gains considerable. An early wander through flower-rich meadows may seem all too short. Easy striding follows, along the tow path of the Macclesfield Canal. Though it passes close to Congleton, you see surprisingly little of the town. Soon, as the canal swings east, The Cloud begins to shadow your progress. You leave the canal just before it crosses what the map calls an 'aqueduct'. However, there's no long series of arches, just an embankment with one short span where the canal crosses over the River Dane. The walk descends slightly to make the river's acquaintance, albeit briefly, before beginning the climb.

This starts with a steady ascent on a lane then continues more steeply, first through pastures and then on rougher slopes clothed in heather and bilberry. The luxuriant growth almost smothers the contours of the old track that once served the quarry on the north face. From a shelf, which extends below the quarry itself, you climb between the crags. This final phase of the ascent is very steep but brief.

You arrive at the northern end of a rocky spine about 100yds (91m) long; the trig point is at the southern end while the highest point is midway along. Sit on the edge of the crags and enjoy the view.

Eastward the ground rises again, into the Peak District. The nearer hills are in Staffordshire. So, for that matter, is the eastern slope of The Cloud, though the summit belongs to Cheshire. Further north, the highest ground is in Derbyshire, though Cheshire claims the western foothills, including the sharp peak of Shutlingsloe (see Walk 12).

THE CLOUD

The western half of the panoramic view from The Cloud stretches over virtually all of the county of Cheshire, is best appreciated from a short way down the descent. Lower down there is a fine pine plantation and some younger woodland. Finally the route drops down the flank of the ridge and into the edge of Timbersbrook.

Silk Industry

In the 18th century Timbersbrook was a centre of the silk industry. The buildings were later taken over by a bleaching and dyeing company. At its height the works employed up to 230 people. It finally closed in 1961 and the mill and chimney were demolished in 1970s.

THE CLOUD

WALK 7 DIRECTIONS

❶ From the car park, turn right for 500yds (457m). Between some brick houses, go left through a gate and down a track. After 600yds (549m) go right through a gate. Follow a trodden line to cross a stream in a dip. Continue diagonally across another meadow. A short embankment leads to a canal bridge.

❷ Cross and loop round left, under the bridge and along the tow path. Follow this for 3.25 miles (5.3km) to bridge 57. Go up the steps and over the bridge. A vague track bears left then swings right through gorse along the edge of a hollow. Descend to a gate then down an often muddy slope to a footbridge. Go through another gate, go down to the River Dane. Turn right on a clear track across a field.

❸ Go through a gate to a road. Turn right and climb steadily. As it levels out, go left on a narrower lane. Opposite a house cross a stile on the right, then continue up fields over a series of stiles, bearing slightly left. Join a lane and go left, past Hillside Farm, then right, up a track to a stile.

❹ There's a National Trust sign, 'The Cloud'. The path is narrow but clear, directly uphill then slanting right. It passes below some crags then levels out and

WHAT TO LOOK FOR
Meadows in the early part of the walk support many wildflowers as well as a variety of grasses. The canal tow path is lined with typical waterside plants, one of the loveliest is meadowsweet – a member of the rose family.

dips slightly to the start of a broad shelf. A path now goes straight up the hillside, through the highest band of crags, to the summit ridge. The trig point is about 100yds (91m) to the left.

❺ Retrace this short section of summit ridge then follow the edge down, gently descending and swinging slowly left. Lower down the path runs through pine plantations. Below a gap in a wall, a broader track runs through more open woods. As the track starts to curve left, a clear path continues ahead. Stick to the crest of the ridge until you rejoin the gravel track near a sharp bend. Just below the bend there's a Gritstone Trail sign and a steeply descending line of steps. Turn left on the road towards Timbersbrook. Just after the first house on the right go through a gap in the fence, down a few more steps and across a field with picnic tables. At its far end is the car park.

WHERE TO EAT AND DRINK
There's no pub in Timbersbrook, but the Coach & Horses is less than a mile (1.6km) along Under Rainow Hill road. It serves Robinson's beer alongside good value food. It's quite small inside but there's a beer garden behind, backing on to open fields.

WHILE YOU'RE THERE
The main radio telescope at Jodrell Bank is usually conspicuous in the view from The Cloud. The 250ft (76m) dish, completed in 1957, has played a hugely important part both in the tracking of space probes and in the understanding of the history of the universe. The story of the observatory and of the science to which it has contributed enormously is told in a fascinating visitor centre.

Trails and Hidden Crags of Frodsham Hill

A short and simple walk on the crest and along the flanks of a prominent red sandstone escarpment.

DISTANCE 3 miles (4.8km) MINIMUM TIME 1hr

ASCENT/GRADIENT 375ft (114m) ▲▲▲ LEVEL OF DIFFICULTY +++

PATHS Clear woodland paths, golf course, 2 stiles

LANDSCAPE Largely wooded steep slopes and gentler crest with a few open sections

SUGGESTED MAP OS Explorer 267 Northwich & Delamere Forest

START / FINISH Grid reference: SJ 518766

DOG FRIENDLINESS Can run free in woodland sections

PARKING Small car park on Beacon Hill, off Simons Lane

PUBLIC TOILETS In Frodsham village

Frosham is at the northern end of the Sandstone Trail, a 34-mile (55km) walk. The sandstone ridge that bounds the western edge of the Cheshire Plain is not completely continuous but does dominate the lowlands along much of its length. In a few places it breaks out into real crags, notably at Beeston (near Walk 4) and at Frodsham and Helsby.

Bare and Bold

Frodsham and Helsby hills form a classic case of what geographers call an escarpment. The strata slope gently down to the south-east: this is the dip slope, while the craggy fronts facing the Mersey are the scarp. The crags of Frodsham mostly lurk among the trees and are only seen at close quarters. Helsby is a different story: its crags are higher and stand out bare and bold in a profile recognisable from many miles away.

Both sets of crags were once popular with climbers. Until the 1970s Helsby was regarded as a crag of considerable significance. Today, however, it is out of favour. One reason, at least according to climbing legend, is the development of a fertiliser factory just downwind! In the case of the smaller crags of Frodsham, once favoured for short practice climbs, the development of artificial climbing walls is probably the most significant factor in their fall from popularity.

In Trust

On Woodhouse Hill, near the southern end of the circuit, there was once a hill fort, probably dating back to the Iron Age. It can be hard to discern the remains now, though it's easier if you go in the winter when they're less obscured by vegetation. This area, and the adjoining Snidley Moor Wood, are now owned and managed by the Woodland Trust, a worthy organisation dedicated to preserving and improving native woodlands for quiet recreation, access and conservation.

After a steep descent the walk returns along the base of the scarp then climbs up through Dunsdale Hollow to the base of the crags. Here you can return to the crest by a flight of steps, though there's an alternative for the adventurous in the steep scramble known to generations of Frodsham people as Jacob's Ladder. Footholds carved in the rock are now so worn that their artificial origin is less obvious. Most people find that the first 20ft (6m) are the most awkward.

Above this the path passes more small crags, some of them eroded into convoluted shapes, before emerging into the open at Mersey View, crowned by the village war memorial. As the name suggests, the grand curve of the Mersey is unmistakable. Hugging the nearer shore is the Manchester Ship Canal, joined almost directly below by the Weaver Navigation. Beyond it you can pick out Liverpool's airport and the city's two cathedrals.

WALK 8 DIRECTIONS

1 Go right along the lane for 100yds (91m), then left down a sunken footpath and over a stile on to a golf course. The path is much older than the golf course and officially walkers have priority, but don't take it for granted! Head straight across and you'll arrive at the 17th tee, where there's an arrow on a post. Drop down slightly to the right, crossing a sandy patch, to a footpath in the trees right of the green below. Bear left at a sign for Delamere

Forest, down a few steps. Keep to the left, passing above crags, then down steps into Dunsdale Hollow.

2 Go left, rising gently, below more crags. At the far end of the path go right then up scratched steps on the corner of the rocks

---

WHERE TO EAT AND DRINK

The Helter Skelter, on Church Street in Frodsham, is named after the centrepiece of the fairground which used to stand on the hilltop, where there's now a modern hotel. The food and beer are excellent and the atmosphere warm and friendly. An alternative, with outdoor seating beneath its vine covered exterior, is Netherton Hall on the A56 west of Frodsham.

---

ahead. Follow a level path through trees, near the edge of the golf course. Soon after this ends, the path rises slightly and passes a bench. After another 20yds (18m), the path forks. Keep straight on along the level path, soon passing a Woodland Trust sign, to a wider clearing with a signpost on the left near the corner of a field beyond.

3 Just before the corner of the field there's a break in a very overgrown old wall on the right, from which a narrow path slants steeply down the slope. There's some bare rock and it can be slippery when wet, so it needs a little care. Near the bottom it turns directly downhill to the bottom corner of the wood. Go

right along the base of the hill. After 800yds (732m) the path twists and descends a little into the base of Dunsdale Hollow. Cross this and go up the other side alongside a stone wall and up a flight of steps. Go right on a sandy track, climbing steadily then passing below a steep rock face.

4 Go left up steps, briefly rejoining the outward route. Jacob's Ladder is just to the left here, up the right-hand edge of the crags. When you reach the top, bear left at a signpost for Frodsham Centre, and follow a sandy track, with occasional Sandstone Trail markers, along the brink of the steeper slope. This passes below some small steep crags before emerging near the summit obelisk.

WHILE YOU'RE THERE

You can hardly ignore the chemical industry, especially from Mersey View, and you can find out more about it at the the Science Discovery Centre in Widnes called Catalyst.

---

5 Turn right just before the memorial on a grassy track (not the path beside the hotel), aiming for telecommunications towers ahead. Go through the ornate iron gates on to the lane and turn right, back to the car park.

WHAT TO LOOK OUT FOR

New red sandstone is about 200 million years old. It is a relatively soft rock, as you can see from the worn footholds of Jacob's Ladder. Curious knobbly shapes in some of the crags often result from wind erosion. Despite strenuous efforts at clearance, rhododendrons remain abundant in parts of the woods. Originating in the Himalayas, they are hardy plants which frequently crowd out native species.

High Rocks of Helsby

The bare crags of Helsby Hill are the highlight of this longer walk.

See map and information panel for Walk 8

> **DISTANCE** 6 miles (9.7km) **MINIMUM TIME** 2hrs
> **ASCENT/GRADIENT** 855ft (261m) ▲▲▲ **LEVEL OF DIFFICULTY** ✚✚✛

WALK 9 DIRECTIONS
(Walk 8 option)

At the clearing (Point ❸), go left along the edge of the wood. At the end turn right on a wider, sandy track and follow it gently downhill. It's distinctly sunken in places. Eventually it levels out and comes out to a lane (Point Ⓐ).

Go right for 350yds (320m) then turn left on narrow Burrows Lane. As it bends left there's a gate on the right with a footpath sign. Follow field-edges to a footbridge and then a kissing gate. Continue, now on the other side of the hedge, to a lane. Go left for 200yds (183m) then right (Point Ⓑ) on a green track.

Follow this green track as far as a kissing gate, after which go right and up a short slope, then round the edge of the field. Go through two further kissing gates and up a fenced path to a lane. Go left and follow the lane to its end then bear left on a track. When it splits, go right and up to the trig point on Helsby Hill (Point Ⓒ).

Though expansive, the view is a mixed bag. Liverpool lies beyond the sweep of the Mersey, but chemical plants, refineries and the M56 clamour for attention. Further away leftwards are the Clwydian Hills. On a clear day, reputedly, you can see Snowdon. The crags below were once very popular with climbers, but have fallen from favour. Apparently the nearby fertiliser plant has made them green and slimy!

Go right, across the top of (but not down) a gully splitting the crags, then steadily down through oak woods. Where the path forks keep right and descend to a stile, then go left down a track signposted 'Old Chester Road'. Lower down the track squeezes between gardens to the street. Go right, then right again on Bates Lane to a footpath on the left, signed 'Woodhouses, Frodsham'. Follow this, then go across a field to a kissing gate.

A few paces ahead is another hedged path. From its end, cross a field and join an old stony track by a ford and footbridge (Point Ⓓ). Go right. The track becomes surfaced. At a T-junction go left 30yds (27m) then right up the drive to The Holt (a house). Just before the gate of the house go left through a kissing gate into the corner of the wood. Walk 8 comes in from above. Go left along the base of the hill and continue to Point ❹ on Walk 8.

Northwich Canals

A gentle walk taking in a stunning piece of Victorian engineering.

DISTANCE 5.5 miles (8.8km)   **MINIMUM TIME** 2hrs

ASCENT/GRADIENT 100ft (30m) ▲▲▲   **LEVEL OF DIFFICULTY** +++

PATHS Woodland paths, surfaced tracks and tow paths

LANDSCAPE Woodland banks, fields, occasional industrial backdrop

SUGGESTED MAP OS Explorer 267 Northwich & Delamere Forest

START / FINISH Grid reference: SJ 653764

DOG FRIENDLINESS Off lead for most of the walk, except in the nature park

PARKING At Marbury Country Park, open till 8pm summer, 5pm winter

PUBLIC TOILETS Close to car park (see walk directions)

WALK 10 DIRECTIONS

The presence of natural brine springs, exploited since Roman times, and of rock salt, mined since the 17th century, made Northwich the cradle of Britain's chemical industry. Directly or indirectly, this has influenced all the landscapes on this walk. The Marbury Estate, the basis of today's country park, was partly built on wealth from salt and was later owned by ICI, who used the hall (which is now demolished) for staff housing.

From the left-hand corner of the car park (as seen when you enter) a gap leads you to an information shelter. Go left up the track alongside an avenue of lime trees. The track bends right, past toilets and the ranger office. Follow it to the next corner, then continue on a footpath to the shores of Budworth Mere and turn right.

Skirt a small 'harbour', which gives a good view across the mere to the sailing club and Great Budworth church, then leave the waterside and go left on a broader path. Follow the main path to a fork and bear left, following a sign 'Anderton Nature Park and canal'. Along here there's a wonderful sculpture (Phil Bews, 2001) made from a fallen tree, as well as lots of rhododendrons. A more open area is good for bluebells in season.

When you come suddenly to the banks of the canal, follow the path round to the right, looping away into the woods. Turn left to reach Marbury Lane. Go left over the bridge and continue down the lane for 0.25 mile (400m), where there's a gate on the right with a sign 'Anderton Boat Lift and Nature Park'. Go down a short

WHERE TO EAT AND DRINK

The Stanley Arms, just up the lane from the bridge above the boat lift, has a beer garden alongside the canal, as well as extensive play facilities. It's also a starting point for boat trips. With a wide-ranging menu too, almost the only thing you can say against it is that it gets a bit busy.

track then detour 50yds (46m) right and up steps to a bird hide, which gives a view over Haydn Pool. Return to the last junction and continue on the path.

Anderton Nature Park was once an industrial site and a variety of waste products – such as salt, lime and ash – create conditions which now allow a tremendous variety of plants to flourish. There's a Wildflower Trail and some of its markers provide useful landmarks for us on this walk.

The path first follows a reed-filled inlet then crosses a bridge. The first marker is No 6, highlighting ramsons and butterbur, well-suited to this riverside habitat. Ramsons is better known as wild garlic and its aroma is very noticeable in spring and summer.

Take the left path here then, at the next junction, slant back right past marker No 4. Go left on the main track and over a bridge to a crossroads, by marker No 3. Orchids grow in the open shade here. Go right, passing marker No 9. At the next junction keep right again, out into an open area, then left at a fingerpost. At a T-junction turn right out into the open, close to the River Weaver, overlooking the soda works.

Just beyond marker No 2, descend some steps, go past the rifle range, and then take a green path away from the river to the dragonfly pond – and another great wooden sculpture. The water here is too salty for fish and frogs to live in, which makes it relatively safe for the larvae of damselflies and dragonflies. If nothing else, throughout the warmer summer months you should see lots of electric blue damselflies, flying low over the water.

Rejoin the main track as it climbs above the river. At the end go through the car park to vist the Anderton Boat Lift. The best views are from the terrace of the café of the visitor centre, but if you want to have a good look round you will will have to allow plenty of time.

Now follow the tow path north to the busy Anderton Marina and on for another 0.25 mile (400m) to the first overbridge after the marina. Go up steps and over the bridge. After 20yds (18m) turn right on a path through woods then at a junction go left (marked 'car park'), looping round into a narrow strip of woodland between the lane and a large pasture.

At a junction with a track, go right signed 'car park' then, after 100yds (91m), go left through a kissing gate. Keep ahead, back to the avenue of lime trees, bear left and left again past the information shelter into the car park and the start of the walk.

WHILE YOU'RE THERE

The Anderton Boat Lift, the first of its kind in the world, represents an ingenious solution to the problem of the 50ft (15m) height difference between the Weaver Navigation below and the Trent and Mersey Canal above. Most of the work was done by allowing extra water into the upper trough, making it heavier than the lower one. With the decline of canal traffic, it became underused and neglected, finally closing in 1983. Restoration of the canal started in 1998 and it's now fully operational once again. A new visitor centre alongside the lift was completed in Spring 2003. Boat trips, several times daily, give you the opportunity to ride in the lift for yourself.

Overleaf: Alderley Edge, Cheshire (Walk 11)

Wizardly Wanderings at Alderley Edge

Layers of history and legend surrounding this famous Cheshire landmark make this short walk a rich mixture.

WALK 11

DISTANCE 3.25 miles (5.3km) MINIMUM TIME 1hr 30min
ASCENT/GRADIENT 445ft (136m) ▲▲▲ LEVEL OF DIFFICULTY +++
PATHS Woodland tracks and paths, some field paths, 6 stiles
LANDSCAPE Woodland, scattered sandstone crags, some farmland
SUGGESTED MAP OS Explorer 268 Wilmslow, Macclesfield & Congleton
START / FINISH Grid reference: SJ 860772
DOG FRIENDLINESS On lead on farmland and always under close control
PARKING Large National Trust pay car park off B5087, closes 5.30pm
PUBLIC TOILETS At car park

There's a lot to take in at Alderley Edge, on the ground, under the ground and even – many believe – in other dimensions entirely.

Ancient Mines and Legends

As long as 4,000 years ago, there was mining activity here, using tools of wood and stone. Mining went on through Roman times but reached its greatest intensity in the 19th century. Copper and lead were the main products, though various other ores were also worked.

Alderley Edge is as rich in legend as it is in minerals. In fact it is probably true that it is rich in legend because of its long history of exploitation. Old shafts and levels or overgrown heaps of spoil can mystify later generations and inspire speculation. Also, working underground, especially in the fickle light of tallow candles or primitive lamps, seems to stimulate the imagination. Waves of immigration, such as those of Cornish miners, import new layers of legend, too.

A Hidden Cave

The most famous legend of the area is alluded to in the names of the Wizard Inn and Wizard's Well, both passed on this walk. Hidden somewhere on the Edge is a cave, guarded by a wizard, in which an army of men and horses sleeps, ready to emerge and save the country when the need is dire. No one has found this cave (though it must be a big one) but you can see the wizard, or at least an effigy, carved in the rocks above the Wizard's Well.

Air of Mystery

This story, and the general air of mystery which often pervades the edge, especially on a misty day with few people about, have inspired many of the books of local author Alan Garner, of which the best known is *The Weirdstone of Brisingamen* (1960).

The walk itself is largely through woodland. In fact the wooded aspect of Alderley Edge is relatively recent. The demand for fuel, building timber and pit props, ensured that the area was cleared of its trees from the

ALDERLEY EDGE

Bronze Age onwards. The local landowner, Lord Stanley, began extensive plantings in the mid-18th century and today the National Trust manages the woodlands carefully. Although Alderley Edge is elevated above the surrounding countryside, its wooded nature means that distant views are rarely unobstructed. From the crest of Castle Rock there is a broad window to the north, towards Manchester with the Lancashire hills beyond, while at Stormy Point the view opens to the east, towards the Peak District.

There are exceptions to the woodland rule. Behind Sand Hills, in the earlier part of the walk, there are shady, damp areas with many orchids, and pools fringed by yellow iris and reed mace (the tall club-headed reed often wrongly called the bulrush). As you near the end, you will be walking though open farmland.

WALK 11 DIRECTIONS

❶ From the car park, just off the B5087, walk towards the tea room and information room. Go right on a wide track past the National Trust works yard, then second left. Cross an open area past Engine Vein. At a crossroads of paths go straight over and come out by Beacon Lodge.

❷ Go straight across the road into Windmill Wood. Follow a gently descending track to a clearing, bear left and continue descending. About 140yds (128m) beyond a National Trust sign,

39

WALK 11

in more open terrain now, with bare sand hills ahead of you, bear right across the grass to a crossroads with a field ahead. Turn right, skirting around some damp ground and then a pool. Just before another open field, go right, along the edge of the wood. Continue in a narrow strip of trees, with fields either side. Cross the road again and follow a track to the bare crest of Castle Rock.

WHAT TO LOOK OUT FOR

Signs of mining activity can be seen in many places, most noticeably at Engine Vein and Stormy Point. There are deep covered shafts within the open working of Engine Vein. Most of what you see today was excavated in the 18th century, but there is evidence of much earlier working. The exposure of bare rock at Stormy Point is partly due to toxic minerals, though wear and tear by the feet of visitors plays a part too.

❸ Descend the steps to a level path. Go left 120yds (110m) to Wizard's Well. Return to the steps and continue below the crags on a terrace path, then up steps to join a higher path. Go left and almost immediately start descending again, with more steps in places. At the bottom cross a footbridge and climb again, levelling out briefly by the Holy Well. A few paces to its left go up over tree roots to where the path resumes. Climb shallow steps to a wider

path, go left then turn right on to the rocky crest of Stormy Point.

❹ Follow the wide level track to a crossroads and go left. Follow signs 'Hare Hill', down a steady descent with a small ravine at the bottom. Turn right and ascend again. Climb some steps past tall beech trees, then descend through Clock House Wood. Climb again to reach a National Trust sign and out into the open.

❺ Go right, over a stile, across the edge of a field to cross another stile. Beyond the pond, go left along the hedge to a stile hidden in a curve, then up a fenced path. Join a wider track and at the top and go over a stile on the right. Go left over the next stile and up to a gate and grassy track. Cross a gravel track into another narrow fenced path and at its end turn left. Opposite the National Trust works yard there's a shortcut to the car park or continue straight on to the tea room.

WHILE YOU'RE THERE

There's a working watermill at Nether Alderley. The building dates from the 15th century though most of the machinery is more recent. It's also a chance to find out exactly why Millstone Grit is so called. The walled gardens and surrounding park of Hare Hill, probably best known for azaleas and rhododendrons, can be reached by a longer walk from Alderley Edge. About 2 miles (3.2km) away, it's fairly well signposted. The gardens are cared for by the National Trust.

Shutlingsloe: the Mini-mountain

A short but intense walk from enclosed valleys and forest to a stark peak.

DISTANCE 5 miles (8km)   MINIMUM TIME 2hrs 30min

ASCENT/GRADIENT 1,129ft (344m) ▲▲▲   LEVEL OF DIFFICULTY +++

PATHS Farm, moorland and forest tracks, 9 stiles

LANDSCAPE Upland pasture, forest, moorland and rocky peak

SUGGESTED MAP OS Explorer OL24 White Peak

START / FINISH Grid reference: SJ 984706

DOG FRIENDLINESS Dogs can run free in forest, sheep elsewhere on route

PARKING Small car park at Vicarage Quarry, Wildboarclough (alternative at Clough House, lower down valley)

PUBLIC TOILETS At Trentabank in Macclesfield Forest, not far off walk route

Shutlingsloe isn't the highest summit in this book, but at 1,660ft (506m) it is one of the highest points in Cheshire, only exceeded by the hills to its east. Of these Shining Tor, on the Derbyshire border, reaches 1,834ft (559m), but – despite its enticing name – it is a shapeless lump by comparison. Shutlingsloe has a special place among Cheshire hills.

A direct approach from Wildboarclough is both steep and short, and doesn't really satisfy. Shutlingsloe deserves better. Devious though it may seem, a loop round through Macclesfield Forest adds substance to the walk and, though still steep in parts, is less drastic than the direct approach.

Macclesfield Forest is also the name of the hamlet that sits in a wrinkle of the hills. Its Forest Chapel dates from 1673 but owes its present appearance to Victorian rebuilding. It was originally a 'chapel of ease' for those who could not regularly make the trek to the parent church at Prestbury. It became an independent church in 1906 and St Saviour's, Wildboarclough, was in turn a subsidiary chapel. The chapel attracts large numbers to its annual rushbearing ceremony, conducted inside the church every August.

Macclesfield Forest provides a source of timber, and the reservoirs provide Macclesfield with most of its water, but it's also important for leisure and wildlife. The dark forest floors under the spruce trees are relatively bare, but the trees themselves are a good place to look for the goldcrest. Although it's Britain's smallest bird, its active habits and bright orange cap make it relatively easy to spot. One of our largest birds, the heron, is also well represented, the colony on the shores of Trentabank reservoir being the largest in the Peak District. Stands of tall foxgloves are seen in recently cleared areas; they are among the first plants to colonise disturbed ground.

The contrast between forest and moors is intense. The path across the moors is well-marked and, for much of its length, has been surfaced with large gritstone flags, and more recycled stone makes the final steep rise straightforward. There's a view indicator just left of the trig point. There's a steep start to the descent but then gradually eases. The waters of Clough Brook once powered a mill, but most of this has now disappeared.

WALK 12 DIRECTIONS

❶ From the car park at Vicarage Quarry, turn left up the road, away from Wilboarclough. Just past Dingers Hollow Farm, go over a stile on the left and up to an iron gate. Go right through a gate and follow a green track across the hillside to a third gate. Cross over a field near a power line, down to a stream then up left to a stile by a gate. Cross the lane and then walk up a few paces to another stile.

SHUTLINGSLOE

A narrow path rises gently beyond, but our route rises more steeply, above large oak and ash trees. Continue to a stile onto a lane. Go right to a junction.

WHERE TO EAT AND DRINK

The Crag Inn, Wildboarclough, is a friendly pub popular with walkers. Built in 1629 and originally a farmhouse, the building has lovely timbered ceilings and wooden settles, and in winter you can relax in front of real open fires. There's a range of home-made food served daily (not Mondays) and children are welcome in the restaurant and garden. Wildboarclough is supposedly where the last wild boar in England was killed.

❷ Turn left, on a lane signposted 'Forest Chapel', over the top and down, with the chapel to your right. Follow the road for 250yds (229m) to a dip. At the corner of a wood go left on a footpath, straight down the hill. At the bottom, near a small dam, take a permissive footpath on the right, signed 'Trentabank'. When a gate blocks the way, drop to the left, down steps to a stile and road.

❸ Cross to a gap in the wall almost opposite. The continuation path parallels the road; when it rejoins it by a gate, bear left on a

WHILE YOU'RE THERE

It's only a few miles over the hill to Buxton, one of England's great spa towns, developed as a northern rival to Bath. The Victorian Opera House is not to everyone's taste, but there's much more unanimous approval for the elegant architecture of the 18th-century Crescent, set against fine formal gardens. On the edge of the town you can venture underground at Poole's Cavern.

wider path, swinging back right. Go up a flight of steps on the left and sharply back left on a path climbing alongside a stone wall. Continue uphill for 0.5 mile (800m) and after a kissing gate bear left on the main path. When you get to the next junction, after about 300yds (274m), go right, with a sign to Shutlingsloe, and up to a kissing gate.

❹ The footpath, partly surfaced with large gritstone flags, crosses open moorland. At a shoulder the path levels out and Shutlingsloe rears up ahead. Descend slightly, and then follow the obvious, flagged path alongside the wall on your right. A final steep staircase leads directly to the trig point.

WHAT TO LOOK OUT FOR

Bilberries can be found in many places, especially along the verges and the edge of the forest. It's a member of the heather family, though the resemblance is not immediately obvious. Small globular pinkish flowers appear from April to July, followed by the blue-black fruits. These are delicious when ripe, but be warned that they were once also harvested for dyes.

❺ Descend straight ahead, winding down very steeply between several low outcrops. Keep straight on as the gradient begins to ease. After crossing a couple of stiles follow a wall down to reach a tarmac track. Go right along this track to a cattle grid then take another track sharply back to the left. This runs more or less level along the hillside, then a gently descending green track interrupted by a stile and a small stream leads down to the road. Go left up this back to the start.

Tegg's Nose Meadows

The set-piece comes early and the rest of the walk unfolds gentler views.

DISTANCE 5 miles (8km) **MINIMUM TIME** 2hrs

ASCENT/GRADIENT 1,152ft (351m) ▲▲▲ **LEVEL OF DIFFICULTY** +++

PATHS Tracks and quiet lanes, some field paths, numerous stiles

LANDSCAPE Steep green hills and valley slopes are main backdrop

SUGGESTED MAP OS Explorer OL24 White Peak

START / FINISH Grid reference: SJ 950733

DOG FRIENDLINESS Can run free in country park, sheep and traffic elsewhere

PARKING Tegg's Nose Country Park pay car park, on Buxton Old Road

PUBLIC TOILETS At car park

The breezy crest of Tegg's Nose, with its interesting quarry remains and fine views, is as far as many visitors get, but a longer walk around the area sets it in context and delivers much greater variety. Although centuries of quarrying have undoubtedly altered the outline of Tegg's Nose, it must always have been a prominent and boldly shaped hill. The beds of massive gritstone that form the summit lie above weaker rocks, which form steep slopes where they're not protected from erosion.

While quarries are a feature of Cheshire and Lancashire, Tegg's Nose is particularly interesting. Examples of preserved machinery, accompanied by explanatory signs, give insights into how the stone was worked. The stone-crusher, for instance, could pulverise around 100 tons of stone a day. Imagine the noise and dust. Ear and lung ailments were common and so were injuries and deaths, from falls and falling rock. Beyond the quarries the track swings round the end of the hill – the 'Nose' itself. The steep slopes add depths to the view south, down to Langley and the River Bollin and across to Macclesfield Forest and Shutlingsloe (see Walk 12). The descent looks west, over Macclesfield and the Cheshire Plain.

The descent is steep, taking you quickly down into woods. Among the beech and oak you'll also find hornbeam. This is often mistaken for beech but its leaves are longer, more pointed and have serrated edges. After crossing Tegg's Nose Reservoir you start to climb again, in the small valley of Walker Barn Stream. Although much of the ascent is on a tarmac lane, it only serves a few farms and is usually quieter than Tegg's Nose itself.

Once over the A537 there's a more level interlude. A bend in the track, where Walk 14 parts company, gives a view down into the valley of the River Dean, sheltered by Kerridge Hill. The village of Rainow was once a silk and cotton weaving centre and a staging point on a mediaeval packhorse route conveying salt from the Cheshire mines.

The A537 has to be crossed again but the final stretch is a pleasure, over easy slopes where, in summer, you're likely to find meadows. High walls, with high stiles, separate them. High walls are usually a sign of abundant stone, often cleared from the fields themselves, rather than quarried.

Prestbury

Bollington
Ⓑ
Redway
Tavern

White Nancy

Bridge
Quarry

Kerridge
Hill

Trig Point 313 ▲
Ⓒ

345 ▲

B5470

Rainow

365 ▲

River Dean

Ⓐ

B5470

BULL HILL LANE

Ⓢ

Hordern
Farm

403 ▲

287 ▲

GRITSTONE TRAIL

Ⓖ

A537

**Walker
Barn**

Ⓐ₄

A537

Macclesfield

0 ———— ½ mile
0 ———— 500m

291 ▲

BUXTON OLD ROAD

❶ Ⓟ 🚻

Clough
House

Tegg's
Nose
Country
Park

380
Quarry (Dis) ●

❷

❸

375 ▲

Ⓟ

Langley
R Bollin

Tegg's Nose
Reservoir

Leather's
Smithy PH ●

WALK 13

WALK 13 DIRECTIONS

1 From the car park entrance a well-surfaced path, almost level, leads off left. At a gate into the country park, go left up steps, past spoil heaps and then below a quarry face. Continue past some old machinery and explanatory signs then above the deep bowl of a quarry. Keep left at the next fork, and follow the main track as it swings round the end of hill.

2 Go left through the second gate, bearing a Gritstone Trail sign. Descend with stone flags on steeper sections, then mostly on grass and through a wood to a small car park. Follow the track across the dam of Tegg's Nose Reservoir then left up a track beside the water. At a fork keep left, down to stepping stones.

3 The track climbs then levels out at a gate just above Clough House. Drop down to a lane and turn left. Follow it up to cross the busy A537 at Walker Barn.

4 Almost exactly opposite is a stile and a track down the hill. Where it starts to bend away right, keep straight on down by a stone wall, over the stream and left to cross a stile. Go left on a grassy path, just above a collapsed wall, then a level terrace path under beech trees. Keep straight

on through the former Hordern Farm, and over a rise until the track bends right. Here are two stiles and various signs.

5 Go left over the first (wooden) stile and along the edge of the field. From a second stile, cross the field corner, bear right to a stile above a steeper slope. Drop down to the stream, angle right then left above holly trees to a stile. Head up past a barn and, from a stile above, bear slightly right and up to Bull Hill Lane. Go left to the junction with the A537.

6 Go left up the main road for about 50yds (46m), cross and go up steps in the wall to a gate

and Gritstone Trail sign. Follow the right edge of the field. The line is now almost straight over a series of stiles, with Gritstone Trail signs all the way, first climbing then levelling out and finally descending before meeting Buxton Old Road. Go right and down, back to the start.

The Bounding Ridge of White Nancy

A sharp ridge, dividing the Cheshire Plain and the upland of the Peak District, is the meat of this longer loop.

See map and information panel for Walk 13

WALK 14

DISTANCE 8.5 miles (13.7km) **MINIMUM TIME** 3hrs 30min

ASCENT/GRADIENT 1,424ft (434m) ▲▲▲ **LEVEL OF DIFFICULTY** +++

WALK 14 DIRECTIONS (Walk 13 option)

At Point **5** go over the second (metal) stile and down the field to join a green track between walls. Bear right over another stile and continue following the wall, then descend a narrowing field above trees. Keep on down the spine of the hill to a tarmac lane, Point **A**.

Bear left to the B5470 and go left until the pavement ends. Cross, descend the track opposite and cross the stream. Climb past ruins and then go straight on walking beside a yound plantation to reach a gate by a large holly.

Just beyond this the path forks: take the lower one, almost level, a little under 0.5 mile (800m) to a fork just beyond a gap in a wall. Keep left, above woodland, and after another 300yds (274m) sidestep right and follow a wire fence. Join a surfaced track and bear left up it. At its highest point, steps climb up to the left, Point **B**. However, for refreshment keep straight on to reach the Redway Tavern, subsequently returning to this point. The steps, then a worn path, climb steeply to White Nancy. This curious, distinctive bell-shaped structure is normally whitewashed but occasionally decorated for special occasions. Paving around it shows the cardinal points.

Head due south along the ridge, transferring to the other side of the wall, to the trig point on Kerridge Hill, Point **C**. The ridge is a sharp dividing line; on the left the Rainow valley and the hills of the Peak District, on the right Macclesfield and the Cheshire Plain. Directly below are fresh quarry workings; compare these raw wounds with those on Tegg's Nose. The path winds through more old workings and then descends a quarry incline and runs out to a lane.

Drop down to reach the main road and then go right for about 100yds (91m). Climb steps alongside a shed, before the first house on the opposite side. Go up the right edge of the field, and out into Bull Hill Lane, then turn right. Walk 13 comes up to the lane just before the junction with the A537 (Point **6**).

Walking to the Mersey Beat

A loop through a great city, starting and finishing on the waterfront.

DISTANCE 3.75 miles (6km)   **MINIMUM TIME** 1hr 30min

ASCENT/GRADIENT 180ft (55m) ▲▲▲   **LEVEL OF DIFFICULTY** ✦✦✦

PATHS Streets and pedestrianised waterfront

LANDSCAPE Great city with wide river views

SUGGESTED MAP OS Explorer 275 Liverpool

START / FINISH Grid reference: SJ 343896

DOG FRIENDLINESS Dogs may not enjoy this walk, need to be kept on lead

PARKING Huge pay car park for Albert Dock complex

PUBLIC TOILETS In Albert Dock complex (and others on route)

WALK 15 DIRECTIONS

Liverpool is ideally suited to exploration on foot. It has the exhilarating sense of space that only harbour cities enjoy, plus a rich history and a unique place in the cultural history of the modern world. Sadly, for many people the name of Liverpool also carries associations with labour problems and riots. Ironically, it was the Toxteth riots of 1981 that sparked a huge effort to revitalise the city, of which the main permanent product was the renaissance of the Albert Dock complex. Dating from 1845, and one of the grandest examples of an enclosed dock anywhere in the world, it's now home to four museums, the Tate Gallery, and a range of shops and bistros to suit all tastes.

From the Britannia Pavilion entrance, beside The Beatles Story, walk through to dockside and turn right. Follow it round and cross Albert Salthouse Bridge, then go right, skirting the Salthouse Dock. Cross the main road at the lights and turn left. Go right into James Street then bear right into the pedestrianised shopping zone of Lord Street, which leads straight into Church Street.

Opposite Marks and Spencer a short side street (Church Alley) leads to the Bluecoat Chambers. Dating from 1717, it's the oldest building, and one of the loveliest, in the city. Return to Church Street, then bear right past the Lyceum Post Office and up long, straight Bold Street, once a centre of rope making. At the end cross to St Luke's Church then turn right on Berry Street. Soon the grand arch leading to Liverpool's Chinatown appears.

Opposite the arch, turn left on Upper Duke Street, and the

WHILE YOU'RE THERE

If you're into the Beatles, don't miss Paul McCartney's childhood home at 20 Forthlin Road (best reached by minibus from Albert Dock). But surely the essential Liverpool experience is a ride on a Mersey Ferry from the Pier Head.

LIVERPOOL

Anglican Cathedral looms into view. Turn left into Rodney Street, right on Mount Street then left on Hope Street. Half-way along is the Philharmonic Hall and opposite is the Philharmonic Hotel, arguably Britain's grandest pub.

Turn left down Mount Pleasant, opposite the Metropolitan Cathedral. Bear right at the bottom past the monumental Britannia Adelphi Hotel, then turn right by the Crown Hotel and then up left into the cavernous train shed of Lime Street Station. This was the terminus of the world's first passenger railway, linking Liverpool and Manchester. Exit the station concourse near the Underground station, out into Lime Street and turn right.

If you can see past the traffic, you now get one of the country's great city views, dominated by the massively elegant St George's Hall. If the exterior is impressive, the interior is awesome. Turn left above it, and down William Brown Street, past the Walker Art Gallery and Liverpool Museum.

Turn left across the bottom of St John's Gardens. Cross St John's Lane and up left then turn right before the Marriott Hotel and under the arch into Queen Square. Go under the canopy then

right down the steps and left into Whitechapel. Follow this down to a pedestrian zone then go right on Stanley Street.

Follow the street along to the Eleanor Rigby statue. Backtrack and then turn into Mathew Street. This street bears slightly right past The Grapes, Cavern Walks, and the Wall of Fame.

At the end, turn left then second right into Lord Street. This leads to Derby Square, the site of Liverpool Castle. Continue up Castle Street towards the Town Hall. Turn left on Water Street then right on Rumford Street.

Turn left on Chapel Street, then diagonally left behind St Nicholas Church. Cross The Strand and go down the side of the Royal Liver Building to the Pier Head. Along with the Cunard and Port of Liverpool Buildings, the Liver forms the great trinity of Liverpool's seafront. The Liver Birds on top, apparently an improbable cross between a cormorant and an eagle, are 18ft (5.5m) high.

Turn left and walk along the Pier Head past the Ferry terminal. Go through a recently redeveloped waterside area that includes the striking new Museum of Liverpool. Continue along Riverside Walk to return to the start at Albert Dock.

WHAT TO LOOK OUT FOR

Liverpool's two cathedrals face each other down the length of Hope Street, but they could hardly be more different. The sandstone Anglican Cathedral is the biggest in Britain and took 74 years to complete. The Roman Catholic Metropolitan Cathedral is far more contemporary in appearance yet was completed (in 1967) 11 years earlier.

Around Lyme Park Without Prejudice

A circuit partly within and partly outside the park itself, climbing to an elevated ridge.

DISTANCE 6.25 miles (10.1km)   **MINIMUM TIME** 2hrs 30min

ASCENT/GRADIENT 886ft (270m) ▲▲▲   **LEVEL OF DIFFICULTY** ✚✚✚

PATHS Stony tracks and moorland paths, some very high stiles

LANDSCAPE Woodland, rough pasture and moorland

SUGGESTED MAP OS Explorer OL1 Dark Peak (southern viewpoint about 100yds (91m) off edge of map)

START / FINISH Grid reference: SJ 963824

DOG FRIENDLINESS On lead in deer park, sheep or cattle elsewhere

PARKING National Trust car park adjacent to house

PUBLIC TOILETS Near tea room, just below car park

It is hard to get near Lyme Park without encountering some mention of *Pride and Prejudice*, though the connection is frankly tenuous. In the acclaimed BBC dramatisation of Jane Austen's novel, Lyme Park stood in for Pemberley, Mr Darcy's home. There is no reason to think that Austen herself had Lyme Park in mind. In the novel, Pemberley is in Derbyshire – and was fictional. But it is a pretty good representation of Jane Austen's description of Pemberley and any excuse for a good walk.

A Wooded Valley

The walk quickly leaves the bustle of the car park for relative tranquillity around Knott – though this can be lively, too, as there's an area where mountain-biking is allowed. The route then descends a wooded valley. The mixture of trees includes Scots pine, sycamore, oak, larch and birch and there are masses of rhododendrons. A good range of woodland birds, from woodpecker to nuthatch, is also present.

Soon the route starts to climb again. Along the first lane are banks of traditional meadow flowers like poppies, ox-eye daisies and cornflowers. Then there's a steady climb through pastureland, punctuated by some self-explanatory place names: Moorside Lane, Keeper's Cottage and Planted Moor. On the last, are several circles of rhododendrons, as obvious and incongruous as any crop circle. Though no one seems to have suggested that these are of extra-terrestrial origin.

Views From the Crest

It's the sort of climb where a rear-view mirror would be useful as the views expand steadily. Alderley Edge (see Walk 11) stands out, with Manchester Airport slightly further away and the whole conurbation beyond. Reaching the crest, there's a new and very different view ahead. The green little valley of Todd Brook, containing the village of Kettleshulme, seems totally enclosed. It actually drains eastward, towards the higher hills of the Peak District which lie beyond. In reasonable visibility the short out-and-back trip along the near-level ridge is highly recommended to open out the view southward. Kerridge Hill and White Nancy (see Walk 14) are conspicuous and the Cheshire Plain sprawls to the west.

You return along the ridge and continue, still virtually level, towards the isolated Bowstones Farm. Just down to the right are the Bow Stones, two shafts of late Saxon crosses. These may have served as landmarks or boundary stones as well as objects of devotion for the local community. The shafts are missing their heads, but these may well be the ones which now reside in the courtyard of Lyme Hall.

You now re-enter Lyme Park and soon descend, with glimpses of the house over the trees. The final section goes through the fallow deer park and then skirts the edge of the gardens, from where you get a classic view of the house reflected by a pool and framed by oak and beech trees.

WALK 16

WALK 16 DIRECTIONS

❶ From the information centre cross the car park and follow the road left, then swing round to the right. Keep right at a fork then straight on up the low rounded hill of Knott. Drop down left to a small car park and through a gate on to a track descending through a wooded valley. Follow this steadily down and out to a lane by West Lodge. Go left, over a bridge, and meet a wider road.

2 Turn left up the track by a chapel. Where it swings right, for Lark Hill, go straight ahead on a level track, then up fields following the Lyme Park boundary wall. Swing right to cross over a small stream, then up and along the crest of a slight ridge. The path acquires a hard surface where it crosses a level marshy area. Go right on Moorside Lane, past Keeper's Cottage, then turn immediately left. Go up alongside a wall to a stile on the crest, then straight down, crossing a green track, to join another track at a gate. Climb again, rejoining the boundary wall. As the slope levels out, the track bears rightwards. One stretch of the track can be boggy, but you'll find there is firmer ground further right.

WHILE YOU'RE THERE

It would seem silly to come here and not visit the house itself. While the exterior is thoroughly 18th century and Italianate (by Giacomo Leoni), much of the original Tudor house survives behind the stone façades. But you won't see any interiors from *Pride and Prejudice*: these were filmed at Sudbury Hall in Derbyshire.

3 Follow a good track southward along the crest of the ridge for 750yds (686m) until the ground falls away. Return along the ridge and continue north along the track, towards the very isolated Bowstones Farm, just before which the track meets a lane. (The mysterious Bow Stones are just down to the right from here.) From the bend of the lane go left following the Gritstone Trail signs, to cross the boundary wall at Bowstonegate. Turn right along the wall and follow it to a corner with a marker stone.

WHERE TO EAT AND DRINK

The National Trust's Coffee Shop in the Timber Yard, on the far side of the large pond, does the usual range of tasty snacks and light refreshments, plus there's a kiosk by the car park for drinks and ice creams. For a wider menu and table service at the Ale Cellar restaurant in the courtyard of the house. Otherwise, there are several pubs in the centre of Disley, less than a mile (1.6km) from the park gates, of which the Ram's Head is probably the best bet.

4 Now descend the slope, swinging left alongside a plantation, with rough steps where it's steepest. Lower down the track forks. The main, left, branch gives an easier gradient but they rejoin at the bottom. Go over a tall stile by the corner of the wall, and down a track flanked by a tall deer fence. Go left through a gate into the fallow deer park. (This may be closed in the breeding season, in which case continue straight ahead, looping round behind the house back to the car park.) Go over a bridge and follow the edge of the gardens round to the right, then descend shallow steps and through a gate back into the car park.

WHAT TO LOOK OUT FOR

Outside the park, you'll see signposts erected by the Peak and Northern Counties Footpaths Society, a voluntary body. The main park has red deer – Britain's largest native mammal – though with 1,400 acres (567ha) to roam, there's no guarantee they'll cross your path. If you get lucky, you can compare the red deer with the smaller fallow deer in their own park.

A Peak Experience Around Dove Stones

A magnificent walk along the edge of the moors is the centrepiece of this grand outing.

DISTANCE 8 miles (12.9km) MINIMUM TIME 3hrs

ASCENT/GRADIENT 1,296ft (395m) ▲▲▲ LEVEL OF DIFFICULTY +++

PATHS Mostly on good tracks but with some rocky sections, occasionally very steep, 2 stiles

LANDSCAPE Open and exposed moors, with sheltered valleys

SUGGESTED MAP OS Explorer OL1 Dark Peak

START / FINISH Grid reference: SE 013034

DOG FRIENDLINESS Condition of access to moors is dogs must be on lead

PARKING Dovestone Reservoir, pay at weekends

PUBLIC TOILETS At car park

Cheshire's stake in the Peak District National Park is modest, but on this walk you can sample the vast moors so characteristic of the Dark Peak. These are notorious for tough walking over peat and heather, but this is an easy promenade along the edge of the moors; the only hard part is the steep ascent of Birchen Clough.

Skirting the Reservoirs

This route starts easily, beside a series of reservoirs, allowing you to look up to the crags on the skyline. Dove Stones, directly above the start, has a natural edge as well as a large, long-abandoned quarry. Above the last of the reservoirs, you follow the Greenfield Brook, climbing gently. The forked tower dubbed the Trinnacle is eye-catching – and you'll get a closer look soon. Don't miss the water-sculpted rocks in the bed of the stream.

The Dark Peak Moors

Now you make the transition from valley to moor, by the steep ascent of Birchen Clough. The steepest step is by a small waterfall and, if it looks uninviting, backtrack a short way to pick up a path (still steep) which traverses above the obstacle. The easier upper reaches of the Clough, and the flanking slopes leading out on to the moor, are home to Canada geese.

You reach the edge of the moor close to Raven Stones and soon find yourself looking down on the unmistakable Trinnacle. It's a great foreground for photographs and looks even better with someone standing on the top, but the ascent can only be recommended to experienced scramblers. You have to sidle along an exposed ledge below the lowest top; then it's easier climbing to the middle one but there's a long stride across a deep gap to the highest – and it seems a lot longer coming back!

Above Dove Stones

The edge is less defined for a time and you cross a vague shoulder past Ashway Cross before clarity is restored. Above Dove Stones the main path keeps back from the edge, but is exposed if you don't mind that sort of thing. Just beyond is the isolated tor of Fox Stone. Here a plaque commemorates two Dark Peak climbers who were killed in the Italian Dolomites.

Rough Shelter

In wild weather, the ruins of Bramley's Cot, once a shooters' hut, provide the best shelter if you need somewhere to take on food and drink. The end wall still stands and you can see the carved sockets where the roof timbers were set. There's still a mile (1.6km) of moor-edge to go before you drop into the valley of the Chew Brook that gives easy walking back.

WALK 17 DIRECTIONS

❶ From the car park walk up to the top of the Dovestone Reservoir dam and turn right, along the road past the sailing club. Where the plantation ends go over a bridge and straight on to follow a private, vehicular track

as it makes its way steadily up to the very top of the Chew Valley.

❷ When you reach Chew Reservoir turn left and walk along by the dam wall until just before it kinks right. With your back to the reservoir (and near a sign warning of the dangers of deep water) drop down to the moorland and follow the very wide, straight track opposite that heads back towards the edge of the hillside. It first bears left, then swings back to the right, and soon becomes a thin path that weaves its way between the loose rocks around Dish Stone Brow.

3 With Dovestone Reservoir coming into view far below, continue along the high rim of the hillside past a series of rocky outcrops. If you occasionally lose sight of the path don't worry, just keep to the wide strip between the steep drop on your left and the banks of peaty bog on your right.

> ### WHAT TO LOOK OUT FOR
>
> As you stand on the edge of the moors above Dovestone Reservoir, taking in the splendid panorama westwards, a small but distinctively pointed hill a mile (1.6km) beyond the reservoir (and topped by a war memorial) tends to catch the eye. It's known as Pots and Pans and its odd-shaped rocks contain weathered holes that were once rumoured to have been specially deepened to hold the wine of well-to-do grouse shooters!

4 Nearing Great Dove Stone Rocks continue to follow the rocky edge as it swings back to the right. Beyond Dean Rocks is a clear path that winds its way around the head of a narrow valley known as Dove Stone Clough.

5 Cross over the stream as it flows over a rocky shelf and, as you continue across the slope on the far side, the narrow path slowly begins to drop down the grassy hillside. Fork left and ignore a higher path towards a prominent stone memorial cross ahead. Soon the path curves

> ### WHERE TO EAT AND DRINK
>
> On sunny weekends the occasional ice cream van is always a welcome addition to the Dovestones car park. Otherwise the nearest place for refreshments is a pub called the Clarence, about a mile (1.6km) away in Greenfield, which serves food daily. For more choice you'll have to try the cafés and pubs of nearby Uppermill.

steeply down to the left and there are numerous criss-crossing tracks through the long grass and bracken. If you are in any doubt then just aim for the unmistakable aqueduct below you, at the foot of Dove Stone Clough, and cross it by using the high footbridge.

6 Walk along the path below the rock face and the fence on your left and across an area of slumped hillside littered with rock debris. Eventually the path joins a wide, grassy strip that gently leads down between fenced-off plantations of young conifers. Go through the gate and drop down through the open field to reach the popular reservoir-side track. Turn left and then follow this track all the way back to the car park.

> ### WHILE YOU'RE THERE
>
> A visit to the Saddleworth Museum and Art Gallery, which is located just 2 miles (3.2km) from Dovestones on the High Street in Uppermill, is highly recommended. The former canalside woollen mill is stuffed full of curiosities and intriguing snippets of local history – from farming to brass bands, Roman soldiers to weaving mills. It's open daily and includes hands-on exhibits for children and informative displays.

Overleaf: Parbold Hill, Lancashire (Walk 18)

Douglas Valley Delights

A gentle yet surprising corner of Lancashire, and it saves the best until last.

DISTANCE *4 miles (6.4km)*   **MINIMUM TIME** *1hr 45min*

ASCENT/GRADIENT *410ft (125m)* ▲▲▲   **LEVEL OF DIFFICULTY** ✦✦✦

PATHS *Field paths and canal tow path, 11 stiles*

LANDSCAPE *Open fields, enclosed valley and wooded dell*

SUGGESTED MAP *OS Explorer 285 Southport & Chorley*

START / FINISH *Grid reference: SD 517109*

DOG FRIENDLINESS *Keep dogs under close control*

PARKING *Large lay-by on A5209*

PUBLIC TOILETS *None en route*

They say West Lancashire is flat, and much of it is, but Lancashire is full of surprises. The walk starts with a slight ascent on to High Moor. Not that it is what we would call a moor today: the name dates back to before the Enclosure Acts. As to the 'high' part, that creeps up on you, unsuspected until you start down an enclosed track and then out into an open field. The spire of Parbold church is below you and, to its right, the land falls away to the real lowlands around Ormskirk and stretching away to the sea.

Napoleonic Fear

Inland you look across the Douglas Valley to the ridge of Ashurst's Beacon which, incidentally, is another grand viewpoint. The beacon was built at the time of the Napoleonic wars, to carry warning of an invasion which many feared was imminent. It was never used.

Leeds and Liverpool Canal

Now you amble down into the valley. Once this was a major communications corridor. First the river itself was improved for navigation in 1742. Then came the Leeds and Liverpool Canal. This was initiated by an Act of Parliament in 1770, but took 46 years to complete. The cost was, a then colossal, £1.2 million. It remains the longest single canal in Britain. It carried stone from local quarries – much of Wigan is built of Parbold stone – and coal from the Lancashire coalfields.

As one of the later canals to be finished, its heyday was relatively brief. The railway between Wigan and Southport, which runs so closely parallel to the canal through the valley, was opened in the mid-19th century. The canal declined but the growth of leisure boating brought a revival.

Fairy Glen

Having climbed up a little from the canal, and crossed a few fields, you come to the pièce de resistance, Fairy Glen. Its origins are largely natural, rather than supernatural, and there are traces of small-scale quarrying, but nevertheless there is a kind of magic about the place. Dappled sunlight gilds the rocks and waterfalls. The ground under the trees, depending when you go, may show celandines and wood anemones, wood sorrel, or carpets of bluebells and wild garlic. Between June and September, especially in the lower reaches, there are drifts of white flowers on loose spikes called enchanter's nightshade – a member of the willow-herb family and not related to deadly nightshade.

WALK 18 DIRECTIONS

❶ At the end of the lay-by there's a stile into the corner of a field. Go up the side of the field and left along the top, then into a wood.

Cross several footbridges and continue up the footpath, then alongside a tiny stream. Follow the side of a conifer plantation until it bends away, then bear right to the left-hand side of a clump of trees

WALK 18

enclosing a pool. Continue up to the right into an enclosed track below power lines and on up to a junction with a tarmac track.

2 Go left, then bear left again down an earthy track. (If you're in need of sustenance and want to visit The Rigbye Arms first, go right at this point, then left along High Moor Lane.) At the end of the earthy track go straight ahead on a fenced path between fields, to the corner of a wood, then over a stile and then down its left-hand edge. Keep following this, which eventually becomes a narrow strip of woodland, to a stile in the bottom corner of the field. Follow a footpath down through the wood then up to the A5209.

3 Cross the road and go left to a stile where the pavement ends.

Go straight down a field and over another stile into a lane. Go right on this then immediately left down another lane. Cross the railway at a level crossing and continue until you reach a bridge over the canal. Drop down to the tow path and follow it left (eastwards) for 0.5 mile (800m) to the next canal bridge (No 40).

4 Cross this bridge and follow an obvious track, taking you back over the railway and up to a junction of tracks. Turn right, on a track past houses, then follow the waymarks for a narrower path alongside a private track. Where this ends at a stile, keep ahead across the large, open field aiming for a post and stile into woodland.

5 Descend the steep steps down into a wood and then bear left into Fairy Glen. Cross a footbridge, climb some steps, then go left up a good track. Cross another footbridge below a waterfall and ascend more steps. Keep to the principal footpath, straight on up the glen as it becomes much shallower, until the path crosses a tiny footbridge. Soon after this the footpath leaves the side of the brook and briefly joins a track before it emerges on to the A5209. Cross and go right, back to reach the lay-by at the start of the walk.

Walking Over Harrock Hill

This extended circuit adds variety and expansive views.

See map and information panel for Walk 18

DISTANCE *3.75 miles (6km)*   MINIMUM TIME *1hr 30min*

ASCENT/GRADIENT *560ft (171m)* ▲▲▲   LEVEL OF DIFFICULTY ✚✚✦

WALK 19 DIRECTIONS
(Walk 18 option)

At the junction with the tarmac track (Point ❷) keep straight on to High Moor Lane. Turn right then, just past the High Moor restaurant, go left up a concrete track. After 600yds (549m) the track curves left.

Keep straight on to a stile, then follow a narrow footpath. Continue walking along the edge of a wood, Point ❹.

Go left, along the edge of the wood, then straight on and up the edge of another wood. Follow it round right, then go left up the edge of the field and into an area of bracken and birch. Go ahead, then left to the gaunt shell of the windmill on Harrock Hill. Its foundations are cut into solid rock. It was active late in the 18th century but fell into disuse by the mid-19th century.

From the ruin of the windmill continue down to the wall, turn right and at the corner of the wood go half-left over a ladder stile. From the next stile there are wide views over the west Lancashire plains. Follow the left edge of the field downhill, then right on a driveway around farm buildings to a lane (Point ❸).

Go left and at the second junction left again. Follow the road uphill for 400yds (366m) and cross a hilltop stile on the right. At the junction of routes by the small car park turn right to follow the broad path along the right-hand side of the fence.

The path skirts the disused Hunter's Hill Quarry. The stone from here, known as Harrock Hill Grit, was highly regarded for its resistance to weathering. It was extensively used for construction around Wigan.

Ignore a path off to the left and instead stay alongside the fence, descending past several houses to a junction (Point ❻). Go left, over a stile between boulders and up the paths. Where the gradient eases there's a signpost on the right. Go down the steps then cross the field to a stile just left of a bungalow. Go left up the lane.

At the top, by The Rigbye Arms, go right on High Moor Lane for about 90yds (82m). Go right down the drive of Stoney Bank House then fork right on a grass path behind a hedge. When this meets another track turn right, rejoining Walk 18 just 100yds (91m) from Point ❷, where you left it.

The Paths to Wigan Pier

A walk to challenge preconceptions, full of wildlife and historical nuances.

DISTANCE 6.25 miles (10.1km) **MINIMUM TIME** 2hrs 15min

ASCENT/GRADIENT 443ft (135m) ▲▲▲ **LEVEL OF DIFFICULTY** ✦✦✦

PATHS Streets, tow paths and good tracks

LANDSCAPE Urban start, semi-urban finish, woodland in between

SUGGESTED MAP OS Explorer 276 Bolton, Wigan & Warrington

START / FINISH Grid reference: SD 579052

DOG FRIENDLINESS Urban start no fun for dogs, but matters improve thereafter, several roads to cross

PARKING Visitor car park Trencherfield Mill

PUBLIC TOILETS Wigan town centre

WALK 20 DIRECTIONS

Many Wigan people still haven't forgiven George Orwell for publishing *The Road to Wigan Pier* (1937). The book was a firsthand account of working-class life in England, but because of the title its grim descriptions have been strongly associated with Wigan. And for many in the Wigan area (and elsewhere) life in the 1930s was grim. Much has changed, as you'll see, not least Wigan Pier.

From Trencherfield Mill, walk out to the main road and turn right (Wallgate) towards the town centre. This gives a poor first impression of present-day Wigan but, as you pass under the railway bridge, an unexpectedly elegant street appears. Follow it up to the part-pedestrianised Market Place and straight on down.

Just before a dual carriageway go right down setts to the former St George's Church, then left and over a pedestrian crossing. Turn right for 30yds (27m) then down left alongside the River Douglas. Follow the path by the river until you reach a turning circle. Cross the left-hand bridge and follow the straight, main track until the tarmac ends in woodland. Descend leftwards with steps, to a bridge over a small stream. Go left on a tarmac track for 50yds (46m) then right just before a bridge.

The track descends to reach the river, rises again and then swings back right. Keep left at a fork. A carved boulder indicates the short track into an old quarry called Devil's Canyon, which is now an adventure playground.

WHILE YOU'RE THERE

There are many attractions at Wigan Pier including the world's largest working mill engine in Trencherfield Mill — an awesome piece of engineering. You can also see working looms in the Machinery Hall. Recent renovations are part of a wider project to redevelop the whole Wigan Pier cultural quarter.

WIGAN PIER

Return to the main track and continue another 60yds (55m) then go left up steps. The path leads past former almshouses known as The Receptacle, then joins a track across fields. Turn right on a lane (Hall Lane) and follow it to Hall Lane Lodge. Go left just before the lodge, then fork right to a canal basin. Iron ore and limestone off-loaded here were carried down a tramway where Hall Lane now runs.

Turn right on the canal tow path to an iron bridge (No 60). Go right, up steps and right again into the shady woodland of Haigh Country Park. Go down the surfaced drive across the old railway, then swing left and down. As it bends back right, go left on a track alongside a brook.

After crossing the stream, go up left to the old railway and turn right. Keep straight on along a wide, well-restored gravel track. On either side are housing estates built on former colliery land.

You emerge at a canal basin in the middle of a flight of locks. There are 21 locks between Wigan Pier and Top Lock. Though the Leeds and Liverpool Canal reached Wigan in 1781, construction of this flight was one reason it didn't reach Leeds until 1816.

The steep mound opposite is known locally as Rabbit Rocks. The short climb to the top earns the widest views on the walk, including Winter Hill eastward and the Peak District due south. The mound is mostly composed of large cylindrical blocks of blast furnace waste – properly known as slag – from the Kirkless Iron and Steel Works, which operated from 1858 to 1931.

The gradual weathering of the slag heap has produced a very alkaline soil, supporting harebells, comfrey and eyebright. The latter has tiny

white flowers with yellow hearts. There are also masses of yellow Oxford ragwort, often covered in the tiger-striped caterpillars of the cinnabar moth.

Return to the tow path and follow it down. Cross the road at Rose Bridge and continue past Whalley's Basin, formerly the junction of a branch canal, now silted up, full of reedmace and popular with anglers.

Cross another road, go under two rail bridges and past the starkly modernist Girobank building. At a canal junction keep to the right branch, and go under the restored Henhurst Bridge.

At Bottom Lock, by Wigan Dry Dock, your starting point is just to the right, but carry straight on to visit Wigan Pier. Go under the next bridge then up and along to a footbridge. Cross this and go left past The Orwell. The original pier, a coal loading stage, was in this area. Finally, retrace your steps to Trencherfield Mill.

Wildlife and Sand at Formby Point

The effort is minimal and the rewards are great on this exhilarating walk through an area of great significance for wildlife.

DISTANCE 3.5 miles (5.7km) **MINIMUM TIME** 1hr 30min

ASCENT/GRADIENT 50ft (15m) ▲▲▲ **LEVEL OF DIFFICULTY** ✦✦✦

PATHS Well-worn paths through woods and salt marsh, plus long stretch of sand

LANDSCAPE Pine forest, sand dunes and a vast sweep of beach

SUGGESTED MAP OS Explorer 285 Southport & Chorley

START / FINISH Grid reference: SD 278082

DOG FRIENDLINESS On lead in nature reserve but can run free on beach

PARKING Either side of access road just beyond kiosk

PUBLIC TOILETS At start

It has to be said that most of the Cheshire and Lancashire coast is fairly urbanised. And as you approach through the town of Formby there's little to suggest that here will be any different. It seems to be somewhere to retire to, or perhaps to commute to Liverpool. This makes Formby Point all the more remarkable.

Tall, shady pine woods form your first impression. They may appear ancient but were actually planted less than 100 years ago, to help stabilise the sand dunes. No one at the time could have suspected that they would become such an important haven for red squirrels. Although recently Formby's red squirrel population has been devastated by a deadly virus, so you will be lucky to spot one.

The dark peaty soils that occur inland of the dunes produce a variety of crops, but a particular local specialty is asparagus. You may still see this growing in the fields that border the reserve early in the walk. On the way out towards the shore you pass a lake, natural in origin, where swans, ducks, coots and moorhens breed.

Miles of Dunes

The sand dunes at Formby forms the largest dune system in England and a vulnerable and precious habitat for wildlife. The line of dunes immediately behind the beach is partly stabilised by the rough-edged marram grass, but high tides and high winds can still change their shape in a matter of hours. The feet of visitors also erode the fragile dunes. The beach itself is littered with patches of shell debris. Under the sand there are many invertebrates which attract wading birds. One of the easiest to recognise is the oystercatcher, which is black and white apart from its bright orange eyes, beak and legs. Many other waders and gulls may also be sighted.

As you walk along below the dunes, you will see some darker layers exposed by erosion of the sand. These sediments were formed around 4,000 years ago, when the shape of the coast was somewhat different. In places they have been found to preserve the tracks of animals and birds, so that we know, for instance, that oystercatchers were plentiful then too. Human footprints have also been found. These suggest that people hunted and fished here, but the most evocative report is of a medley of small prints suggesting children at play.

A Haven for Wildlife

From the end of the beach you wind through the sand hills again, past pools where natterjack toads – one of Britain's rarest animals – breed. Two other rarities that are also found here are great crested newts, around the pools, and sand lizards, in the drier areas.

WALK 21 DIRECTIONS

❶ Start just left of the large notice board. Follow the 'Squirrel Walk', with its wooden fencing, to the left and then round to the right. Keep straight on at several crossroads. There are many

subsidiary paths but the main line runs virtually straight ahead to Blundell Avenue. Cross the avenue to a fainter path almost opposite, with a 'No Cycling' sign and traces of bricks in its surface. Follow this, skirting around the edge of a field (brick traces are still a useful guide). Go up a slight rise then across more open sand hills to a line of pines on a rise ahead. Skirt left round a hollow and you will see houses on the edge of Formby ahead.

2 Just before reaching the houses turn right on a straight track. This swings left slightly then forks. Go right, down steps, then straight on down the side of a reed-fringed pool. Go straight on, over a crossroads towards the sand hills. When you reach them swing left then right, picking up a boardwalk, to skirt the highest dunes and so out to the beach.

WHAT TO LOOK OUT FOR

If you are very lucky you might see a red squirrel or a natterjack toad. Once prevalent in these parts, sightings are now rare.

3 Turn right along the open and virtually level sand. The firmest walking surface is usually some way out from the base of the dunes. Walk parallel to these (heading north) for over 1.25 miles (2km). The shoreline curves very gently to the right but there are few distinctive landmarks apart from yellow-topped signs to various approach paths. It would be all too easy to just keep on going, so watch for a sign for the Gipsy Wood Path.

4 A distinct track winds through sand hills then swings more

WHERE TO EAT AND DRINK

The Freshfield Hotel (turn left at the junction about 400yds/366m east of the level crossing) only serves its good-value food at lunchtimes. This could be a good reason to time your visit accordingly, especially if you're a lover of real ale. At other times, or if you've children in tow, try The Grapes, at the other end of Massams Lane.

decisively to the right near some pools, where there's a sign board about natterjack toads. Follow the track back into woods and, at a junction, go right. The route curves round between woods and sand hills then joins a wider track by a Sefton Coastal Footpath sign. Go right through a patch of willows then bear left to a line of pines on a rise. From these drop down to a broad path with a gravelly surface and follow it left into woods again. Stick to the main path, with timber edgings and white-topped posts, bear right by a large 'xylophone', and continue quickly back to the start of the walk

WHILE YOU'RE THERE

One way to get to Southport would be simply to keep walking along the sands. It's a resort that retains much of the genteel flavour of its Victorian heyday. Amenities are largely as you'd expect, with a boating lake and amusement park, a small zoo and an aviary in Hesketh Park. At low tide the sea can be miles away and instead of windsurfers you'll probably see land yachts.

Lancashire's 'Fens' and Martin Mere

An easy walk on the West Lancashire Plain, under wide skies, around a great bird centre.

DISTANCE 5 miles (8km)   MINIMUM TIME 2hrs

ASCENT/GRADIENT 50ft (15m) ▲▲▲   LEVEL OF DIFFICULTY ✦✦✦

PATHS Canal tow paths, lanes, farm tracks and field paths, 4 stiles

LANDSCAPE Flat and open farmland with glimpses of wilder wetland

SUGGESTED MAP OS Explorer 285 Southport & Chorley

START / FINISH Grid reference: SD 423126

DOG FRIENDLINESS On lead across farmland but can be let off on tow path

PARKING Several small lay-bys near mid-point of Gorst Lane

PUBLIC TOILETS None near by, unless using Martin Mere Visitor Centre

The levels of south-west Lancashire seem to provide easy travelling: there are miles of canal with no locks and roads and railways with scarcely an incline – and there's easy walking too. However, for most of history these lowlands were an obstacle. Ancient roads and trackways follow the high ground because, until well into the 18th century, this gave easier and faster travelling.

The Lancashire Mosslands

The Industrial Revolution was closely paralleled by, and to some extent depended on, an agricultural revolution. In many cases the same engineers who built the great canals were also responsible for great drainage schemes. The flat peat Lancashire mosslands were largely transformed into farmland. They fed the growing towns elsewhere in the county with green vegetables, carrots and, above all, potatoes.

Only a few pockets of mossland survive in anything like their original state. Leighton Moss (see Walk 49) is one and the Martin Mere reserve, once a lake, possibly the largest in Lancashire, is another. It's no accident that both are now centres of importance for wildlife and birds.

Wildfowl Reserve

Martin Mere Wetland Centre is one of nine in the UK run by the Wildfowl and Wetlands Trust, founded by Sir Peter Scott. The reserve itself plays host to a wide variety of resident and migrant birds. Breeding species range from reed and sedge warblers and reed buntings to the graceful-looking avocet. However, it's the massive flocks of winter visitors that create the most spectacular displays.

The reserve is merely a kind of nucleus and great numbers of geese and swans gather on the fields around, often partly flooded in the winter months. A particular feature is the large number of pink-footed geese – but don't assume that geese with pink feet are necessarily pink-footed geese! They might be greylags – but these are larger and heavier, with longer bills, and may be seen all year round.

MARTIN MERE

Please note that the Wildfowl and Wetlands Trust has waymarked a concessionary path around the south of the reserve from where you can enjoy the birds without disturbing them. This is particularly important when huge flocks of geese gather over winter. The reason is that if disturbed the birds may settle further away, on land owned by less sympathetic farmers, and risk being shot. The ground can be wet at this time of year and you might find the walk more comfortable in wellies.

WALK 22 DIRECTIONS

❶ Near the mid-point of Gorst Lane there's a small timber yard. Follow a short track up through this to meet the canal by an old swing bridge. Go right along the tow path and follow it for about 0.75 mile (1.2km) to Gregson's

Bridge. Go under the bridge then continue up to a lane.

❷ Go left and join a wider road (Martin Lane) and follow it away from the canal for about 350yds (320m). At a bend, by the Martin Inn, bear right down a narrow lane. Follow this for about 700yds

MARTIN MERE

(640m), past the tea rooms at 'The Farm, Burscough', to a very open section. Opposite some glasshouses there's a footpath sign on the right. Follow the track to the railway line.

3 Cross the line and continue down the track until you come to a green shed. Go right, alongside a drainage ditch, until another ditch appears ahead. From here go right and then left on a waymarked concessionary route around the edge of Martin Mere Reserve. It's a clear and easy track that at one point has a viewing position into the heart of the reserve. Keep to the outer edge of the embankment and eventually swing left. Beyond a gate follow the edge of a high, straight fence to reach the road. (Turn left here to reach the main entrance to the reserve, about 400yds/366m further along.)

4 Turn right and follow the road for 500yds (457m). About 100yds (91m) past Brandreth Barn you will see a footpath sign on the right. Go along this as far as a large shed and turn left, past a pool, and on down an obvious track across wide open fields.

5 When you reach the end of the track, just before a lane, turn right on a concrete track. Then, turn right before a house and follow the fence round to

the left. Keep almost straight on ignoring a signpost pointing right, and cross the field straight ahead aiming towards a couple of trees. These act as direction posts down the field-edges to the railway line. Cross and keep straight on, following the slightly raised line of old field boundaries, then join a track to, and then through Crabtree Bridge Farm.

6 Swing right on the tow path. It's about 200yds (183m) to the swing bridge by The Farmers Arms and another 500yds (457m) to the smaller one above the timber yard. Drop back down through this to Gorst Lane.

A Hidden Gem: Healey Dell

This is the shortest walk in the book, but it packs a lot in.

DISTANCE 2.5 miles (4km)   MINIMUM TIME 1hr

ASCENT/GRADIENT 640ft (195m) ▲▲▲   LEVEL OF DIFFICULTY +++

PATHS Field paths, old railway line and surfaced tracks, 5 stiles

LANDSCAPE Open fields, enclosed and densely wooded valley

SUGGESTED MAP OS Explorer OL21 South Pennines

START / FINISH Grid reference: SD 879155

DOG FRIENDLINESS Can roam free in Healey Dell but not on grazing land

PARKING Parking by Healey Dell Nature Reserve Visitor Centre

PUBLIC TOILETS By junction of A671 and B6377, near access road

---

Healey Dell is a gem, and so unexpected. It is packed with delights in a small compass. You could spend hours exploring. And although it is a short walk, its twists and turns make it longer than it looks on the map.

In classic Lancashire fashion, what was once an industrial site is now a haven for wildlife, although the industrial archaeology adds an extra dimension. The fast flowing River Spodden carved the gorge down through the gritstone beds, harder strata creating a number of waterfalls. It also provided a power source for a succession of mills, from early ones grinding corn to later wool and cotton mills.

Near the start of the walk, where the valley is wider, several substantial mill buildings remain. One of these now houses the visitor centre which has exhibitions on the industrial heritage of the reserve. Even in the very tight confines further up, mills were constructed on what must have been very awkward sites, but were unable to compete with larger factories and steam power. The Dell is crossed by the former Lancashire and Yorkshire Railway line. You come down to this line, from the open fields above, close to the site of Broadley Station, where platforms still survive. You follow it through regenerating woodland, feeling quite enclosed, before suddenly bursting out on to the viaduct at treetop height. This impressive eight-arched structure, 100ft (30m) high and 200ft (61m) long, was completed at considerable cost in 1880, but the line was never an economic success.

From its far end you drop down steeply into the shady Dell. Some tumbledown walls remain and a couple of frail-looking arches span the rushing stream. Illustrations from a century ago show these arches still supporting the walls of a two-storey building. Just below, almost directly under the pillars of the viaduct, is an old sluice and the start of the water-cut that fed the great mill pond lower down. You follow the cut down until it disappears into solid rock. This tunnel, probably carved out with nothing more than hand tools, is another example of the extraordinary efforts that were needed to exploit this tricky site. The mill pond itself is now colonised by anglers. As you descend below its retaining wall you get an idea of the depth of water – the head – that it provided to the larger mills just below.

▲ 401

Rooley
Moor Brow

B

*Naden
Higher Reservoir*

Naden
Head

Top
of Pike
398 ▲

ROOLEY MOOR RD

A

Reddyshore

375
▲
Warm
Slack
Hill

Quarries
(disused)

*Spring Mill
Reservoir*

C

Forsyth
Brow

Whimsy
Hill

318
▲
Hunger
Hill

Prickshaw

❸

Knack's
Farm

Broadley
Station
Platforms

Smallshaw
Farm

🅿

❷

4

A671

229
▲

Healey
Dell

5

Cascades

0   ¼ mile
0   500m

🅿

❶

Old Railway

A671

Visitor
Centre

↓ Rochdale

WALK 23 DIRECTIONS

1 With your back to the visitor centre, turn left and walk past the first range of buildings. Cross a gated bridge and turn right. Take the lower path, along the river, past more overgrown ruins. Near a green footbridge go sharp left up the bank then right, along the edge of a clearing, and back into woods. Go left just before a stream on a narrow path, climbing steeply in places. Stone flags help over a wet patch before the path dips to cross the stream. Climb again on the other side and join a broader green track. Where this narrows, go over a stile and up the edge of a field to Smallshaw Farm.

2 Go left before the first building then through a gate into the yard. Go left on a track to a road. Go right and up to a bus turning circle. Turn right opposite this along a track. Follow this for 400yds (366m) to Knack's Farm.

3 Continue over a cattle grid and down a lane, then fork right on a track. After a slight dog-leg the track becomes greener. Follow it round left and back right, then over a stile ahead and down a field by a fence and a ruined wall. Go over a stile at the bottom, down to a lane and go left a few paces.

4 Go down a ramp and steps to an old railway line. Turn right along it for 500yds (457m) then

cross the viaduct high above the Dell. Go left down steps to the access lane, under the viaduct then sharply back right on a broad path. Where this starts to level out there's a 4-bar stile on the left. But first walk a short way upstream in order to see the cascades.

5 Return to the stile and cross it. Follow the stone setts (often slippery) down to a sharp bend, with more remains just down and right. From the bend a footpath follows the tops of some old walls then curls down steeply to a weir. Step across the water-cut on some stone slabs and follow it down. When it enters a tunnel carved in solid rock, the footpath goes to the right. Almost opposite a tall pillar it swings away from the river and out past a terrace of houses to the lane. Go down this below a tall brick retaining wall and back to the start.

The Cotton Famine Road

A longer circuit on to Rooley Moor makes for a dramatic contrast.
See map and information panel for Walk 23

DISTANCE *5.5 miles (8.8km)* **MINIMUM TIME** *2hrs*
ASCENT/GRADIENT *1,180ft (360m)* ▲▲▲ **LEVEL OF DIFFICULTY** ✦✦✦

WALK 24 DIRECTIONS
(Walk 23 option)

From the turning circle go straight up the hill on a setted track, and then a rougher section. As the gradient eases branch left, under pylons, then swing left before turning right on a track rising across Forsyth Brow. Near the corner of the wall, the track goes straight on then levels off below a steep eroded face at Reddyshore, (Point **Ⓐ**). Over to your left are massive wind turbines.

The path meets a wall near the ruins of Naden Head. Follow the wall up and into a dip, then bear right up an open slope. Keep straight on up to meet the Rooley Moor road again. The well-laid setts date from a relief project during the Cotton Famine of 1862–3, which resulted from supply interruptions during the American Civil War.

Go left for about 300yds (274m) to the ruins at Rooley Moor Brow (Point **Ⓑ**). Near by, until the 1930s, was the Moorcock Inn. Rooley Moor may be deserted today, but within living memory it supported dozens of working quarries, plus several small collieries on the Rossendale side. Skylarks are plentiful on these moors, yet relatively unfamiliar bird to most of us. Small,

brown, and inconspicuous, they are usually heard before seen, which means that where there is background noise they often go unnoticed.

Backtrack and follow the road down, rising slightly across the shoulder of Top of Pike. As the road descends again, there's a splendid view over Rochdale towards the northern hills of the Peak District. The descent becomes steeper, and rougher.

Below a short section of restored setts (Point **Ⓒ**), go left on a track that rises slightly. As it levels and swings further left, cut straight down past old stone pits to another track, part of the old tramway system that served the quarries. It soon swings straight down the slope, continuing alongside a wall and heading to the left of two tiny reservoirs. Follow it down between walls, then descend a short flagged section of track to the restored cottages of Prickshaw.

Turn left and then right below the lower houses and onwards down the track. This passes a reservoir, then levels out. Opposite the car park go left down a ramp and steps, rejoining Walk 23 at Point **❹**.

Wayoh and Entwistle

To moorland, then around several reservoirs that are havens for wildlife.

DISTANCE *4.25 miles (6.8km)* MINIMUM TIME *1hrs 30min*

ASCENT/GRADIENT *295ft (90m)* ▲▲▲ LEVEL OF DIFFICULTY +++

PATHS *Mostly on good tracks, 4 stiles*

LANDSCAPE *Rough pasture on edge of moors, wooded watersides*

SUGGESTED MAP *OS Explorer 287 West Pennine Moors*

START / FINISH *Grid reference: SD 722173*

DOG FRIENDLINESS *Reasonable scope for dogs to run free around reservoirs*

PARKING *Batridge Barn pay car park*

PUBLIC TOILETS *Nearest at Jumbles Country Park, 3 miles (4.8km) away*

WALK 25 DIRECTIONS

Tucked into the moors north of Bolton is a string of reservoirs. The oldest, Entwistle, was completed in 1838, originally to serve the mills and bleach works in the valley. Today, together with Wayoh (1876), they supply around half of Bolton's water. Unlike the country park at nearby Jumbles Reservoir, Entwistle and Wayoh are enrobed in mature woodlands with plentiful wildlife.

Be aware that there are two car parks for Entwistle Reservoir, close together but with separate access roads. From the far end of the car park a footpath rises to the right. Go up steps and over two stiles, cross the access road to a gate then cross a rushy pasture to the road. Go right 100yds (91m) to a track on the left by a public footpath signpost.

The track gives easy walking, generally downhill, for almost a mile (1.6km). About 300yds (274m) beyond Clough House Farm, go through a gate on the

WHERE TO EAT AND DRINK

The Strawbury Duck has a great selection of beers, good food including a decent vegetarian choice, outside seating and is open all day. It was originally the Station Hotel, built around 1900 and extended in 1981 into the much older cottage next door.

left and down a green track above a little valley. This passes a small and now derelict mill.

Just below this, cross the Bolton-to-Blackburn railway at a level crossing. The station has long been closed, with new housing replacing the old station buildings, platforms and yard. Continue, down a lane of fine setts. At a fork go left up a gravel track, to emerge into Chapeltown High Street at the side of the Chetham Arms. (The Chethams, a Manchester merchant family, once owned nearby Turton Tower – see information panel on next page.) Don't overindulge, as you'll shortly be passing the former Police Station.

ENTWISTLE

Turn left. The street is a harmonious collection of fine stone buildings. The name 'Chapeltown' seems a little odd, as the village is actually dominated by the spire of St Anne's Church (which serves the whole Edgworth parish), with not a chapel in sight. Continue through a short section with no pavement then turn right on Embankment Road. Go down through the gap, right of a set of gates inscribed 'Wayoh Reservoir', and straight down to Wayoh dam.

It's worth going a short way out on to the dam to see the elaborate intake on the left and impressive spillway down to the right. Just before the dam a broad track follows the shoreline, mostly through plantations but with plenty of open views. You're encouraged to keep to the track to allow the wild flowers to flourish. There are many birds here too, in the woods and on the water.

After about 0.75 mile (1.2km) bear right on a causeway, from where there's a good view of the impressive railway viaduct, often mirrored in the sheltered waters. At the end of the causeway keep right, still following the shore, swinging round through open plantations. At the end go up slightly then turn right and follow the road across another dam/causeway. Turn left on another good path on the further shore.

The path generally runs a little away from the water to avoid disturbance to the vegetation along the margin. This upper reach of Wayoh Reservoir is particularly important in conservation terms, supporting many plants typical of damp areas. One of the more conspicuous is hemp agrimony. It has spear shaped, rough-edged leaves and flattened clusters of tiny pink flowers.

Just above the head of the lake cross the river on a footbridge. After a second footbridge, with a 'canal' upstream of it, there are several paths. Go straight ahead, right of a bench. The path then swings left as it starts to climb, steadily through the trees. Many years ago, when the sounds of industry echoed around these parts, an overhead cableway stretched down the hillside at this point, linking Entwistle Station to a bleach works lower in the valley.

Leave the trees and go up the field to a gate. Go right up the lane and over the railway bridge. Just beyond are Entwistle Station and the Strawbury Duck. There's a footpath sign left of the pub. Follow the lane in front of a terrace of railway houses. After passing a few more houses the lane slips down to the dam of Turton and Entwistle Reservoir. Cross this to return to the car parks at the start – go up and right to reach Batridge Barn.

Walking Ways on Blackstone Edge

A steady climb to a rocky ridge on the Pennine watershed.

DISTANCE 6.5 miles (10.4km)   **MINIMUM TIME** 2hrs 30min

ASCENT/GRADIENT 1,066ft (325m) ▲▲▲   **LEVEL OF DIFFICULTY** +++

PATHS Field paths, rough tracks and faint paths across open moorland, 2 stiles

LANDSCAPE Sheltered valley, rough pasture, bleak and rocky moors

SUGGESTED MAP OS Explorer OL21 South Pennines

START / FINISH Grid reference: SD 940153

DOG FRIENDLINESS Most of walk on grazing land, so dogs under control

PARKING Hollingworth Lake Visitor Centre pay car park

PUBLIC TOILETS At visitor centre

Is it or isn't it? Even the experts seem to be divided. It seems fairly clear that there was a Roman road across the Pennines linking Manchester (Mamucium) with what is now Ilkley, in West Yorkshire. And there certainly is an old road over Blackstone Edge Moor. However the stone surface which can still be clearly seen is much more recent and so are the carvings on the Aggin Stone. The route was well-used by packhorse trains and other travellers in medieval times and only faded into relative obscurity with the advent of canals, turnpike roads and railways.

Old Trading Route

The best guess of the age of the existing masonry is probably less than 200 years. This may seem a let-down if you're sold on the Roman connection and want to add another nought, but on reflection it's still quite impressive. And those old stones are highly evocative, whether you choose to imagine Roman legionaries tramping up the steep incline, or 15th-century merchants and their trains of horses laden with bales of wool or barrels of salt. Romans or merchants alike would surely have regarded these high, exposed moors as an awkward obstacle to be surmounted, not as an attraction to be sought out.

The Pennine Way was the first long distance path to be proposed in the UK and the first to be opened: it was officially inaugurated in 1965. It stretches from the Peak District to the Scottish Borders. In fact, it's topped and tailed by pubs: the Old Nags Head in Edale and the Border Inn, Kirk Yetholm. In between lie 268 miles (431km) of walking and the stretch over Blackstone Edge is a fair sample.

The huge popularity of this walk route has created problems with erosion in a number of places. In fact stories about erosion may have contributed to a decrease in the numbers tackling it, though the main factor is the great expansion of a network of other long distance paths, from the South West Coast Path to the West Highland Way. These days far greater concerns about erosion result from the inappropriate and often illegal use of motorbikes and four-wheel drive vehicles.

BLACKSTONE EDGE

The rocks of Blackstone Edge stretch for about 0.5 mile (800m) and have some appeal for rock climbers. The main climbing area is north of the trig point where there are about two dozen routes. Of course this walk is not solely about the ridge. It starts and finishes in softer country dotted with old farms and weavers' cottages. At Syke Farm, near the end, there's another ancient lane. And the hill just above is called Benny Hill, which will amuse some people hugely and others not at all.

WALK 26 DIRECTIONS

❶ From the far end of the car park a path runs past picnic tables then crosses and follows a small beck. At a track go left 200yds (183m) then up right with yellow arrows. Zig-zag up the slope then left and down to a stream and footbridge. Where the path forks keep to the lower one, just above the stream. It wriggles through birch woods then up to a wider path and round to Owlet Hall.

2 Go through a small wooden gate and left alongside the house to a stile. Cross the stream, and then another stile. Ignore the path on the left and keep right, just above the stream, along a line of thorn trees. Cross a decrepit fence and follow a neglected path alongside a wall. Go up to the trees flanking the drive to Shore Lane Farm. Turn left, then left again on a lane.

3 Just before a road, turn right on a track to walk past some houses. Continue on a narrower but clear path. Meet a farm track just below the A58, go right a few paces, then left up the well-worn path, a former Roman road. Cross a water-cut and then keep on climbing. The slope eases near the Aggin Stone.

4 Turn right, through a kissing gate and follow a rough path across a rock-strewn moor to the trig point. Follow the main edge south for another 400yds (366m) to a break in the line of rocks.

5 Slant down right across rough moor to the old water-cut. Go left alongside this until the path veers off right. The path soon rises again, across a shoulder of moor, then levels off by a small cairn. Keep right, along the edge, descend more steeply then swing right, joining an old grooved track. Continue down a green track, past a cairn, then back left descending towards Dry Mere.

6 Where the ground steepens, just beyond the tarn, the path splits. Take the lower one, towards a pylon. Go straight across a well-used track to another track just below. Go left, fording a small stream, then swing right. Drop down to a shale track in a small valley and go right down it.

7 At Syke farm join a surfaced lane. At Hollingworth Fold, with its multicoloured signpost, just keep ahead down the lane to join the road along the lake side. The entrance to the visitor centre is just across the first embankment.

Rocks and Water at Anglezarke

A landscape shaped by quarries and reservoirs, full of interest both historical and natural.

DISTANCE 7.25 miles (11.7km)   MINIMUM TIME 2hrs 45min

ASCENT/GRADIENT 689ft (210m) ▲▲▲   LEVEL OF DIFFICULTY +++

PATHS Mostly good tracks with some field paths, 16 stiles

LANDSCAPE Woodland, reservoirs, open valleys and farmland

SUGGESTED MAP OS Explorer 287 West Pennine Moors

START / FINISH Grid reference: SD 621161

DOG FRIENDLINESS Can run free on reservoir tracks, sheep elsewhere

PARKING Large car park at Anglezarke

PUBLIC TOILETS Nearest at Rivington (see Walk 30)

A string of reservoirs moats the western side of the high moors of Anglezarke and Rivington and quarries scar their flanks. This is not a pristine landscape by any stretch of the imagination, yet today it is seen by many as an oasis of tranquillity close to busy towns and a motorway.

Reclaimed by Nature

A gentle start just above the shores of Anglezarke Reservoir leads to Lester Mill Quarry, which was worked until the 1930s. The quarry wall is imposing, but somewhat vegetated, and the rock is loose in places. It is much less popular with climbers than Anglezarke Quarry. The name is one reminder that this valley was once a thriving agricultural community. The mill, which served the whole valley, was drowned by the reservoir in 1855. Cheap imports further weakened the rural economy. Today there is only one working farm east of the reservoir.

The route continues through a mix of woodland and pasture to the head of the water, then heads up the valley below steep, bouldery Stronstrey Bank. There's another quarry high on the right near the end of the bank, seemingly guarded by a number of gaunt, dead trees. Further on is another, set further back. Just beyond this an impressive spillway testifies to the potential power of Dean Black Brook.

A Busy Industrial Village

Now you cross The Goit, a canal that feeds the reservoir, to White Coppice cricket ground. There's a small reservoir just above and you pass others on the way down to the present-day hamlet. These served the mills that flourished here for well over a century. Along with the quarries at Stronstrey Bank these made White Coppice a busy industrial village with a population which may have approached 200. The mill closed in 1914 and little remains today. The railway closed in the late 1950s, the school in 1963 and the church in 1984. This sounds like a story of decline yet today many people would see White Coppice as an idyllic place to live, a fact reflected in the local house prices.

ANGLEZARKE

View to Winter Hill

After White Coppice you climb to Healey Nab. Trees obscure what must have been a fine all-round view from the highest point, but there's a good southward prospect from the large cairn on Grey Heights. Winter Hill is the highest of the moors, unmistakable with its TV towers. The main mast is just over 1,000ft (305m) tall, so you could argue that its tip is the highest point in Lancashire. The string of reservoirs is also well displayed and you get a bird's eye view of Chorley.

The walk finishes across the Anglezarke dam and then, to minimise road walking, makes a short climb to the small Yarrow Reservoir. The final descent gives an opportunity to look into Anglezarke Quarry.

ANGLEZARKE

WALK 27 DIRECTIONS

1 Leave the car park on the signposted 'Anglezarke Trail', then follow the 'Woodland Trail' through Lester Mill Quarry. At a junction go right, and ahead at the next junction, climbing steeply.

2 Go through a gap on the left, on a bend. The path traverses a wooded slope. Descend steps, join a wider track and go left. Beyond a kissing gate follow a narrower path until it meets a road.

3 Go left 50yds (46m) to a kissing gate. Follow a track up the valley below Stronstrey Bank. Cross a bridge then go through a kissing gate to reach White Coppice cricket ground.

4 Bear left up a lane, then follow tarmac into White Coppice hamlet. Cross a footbridge by the post box. Follow a stream and then go up left by a reservoir. Bear left to a stile. Cross the next field to its top right corner and then go right on a lane. Where it bends right go left up a track.

5 Skirt Higher Healey, follow field-edges, then angle up left into dark plantations. Fork left just inside, and ascend to an old quarry entrance. Keep left on the main path around it, drop down through woods and up to a gate. Go right at the crossroads and up the woodland edge.

6 At the top turn left for the large cairn on Grey Heights. Descend to the right on a path, near the wall, and at a junction go left, over a stile. Eventually a track leads to White House farm.

7 Cross a stile on the left, below the farmyard wall, then bear left to the corner of the field. Cross the stile on the left then up the field-edge and join a confined, fenced path. From a stile on the right follow trees along the field-edge to a rough track. Go right and straight on to Kays Farm.

8 Go right on a track then left on a lane below the reservoir wall. As the lane angles away, go left over a stile then skirt the reservoir until pushed away from the water by a wood. Join the road across the dam. Go through a gap and up a steep track. Go left at the top round Yarrow Reservoir to a road.

9 Go left, passing the entrance to Anglezarke Quarry, to a junction. Go right, and the car park entrance is on the first bend.

The Deserted Valley of Haslingden Grane

A walk which, more than most, lays bare the past.

DISTANCE 3.5 miles (5.7km) **MINIMUM TIME** 1hrs 30min

ASCENT/GRADIENT 426ft (130m) ▲▲▲ **LEVEL OF DIFFICULTY** ✦✦✦

PATHS Good tracks, a few steep and rough sections, 5 stiles

LANDSCAPE Rough pasture and moorland, some woodland

SUGGESTED MAP OS Explorer 287 West Pennine Moors

START / FINISH Grid reference: SD 752232

DOG FRIENDLINESS Mostly grazing land, dogs under control

PARKING At Clough Head Information Centre car park (locked 5pm), B6232

PUBLIC TOILETS In information centre

It's hard to believe today, but the Grane Valley was once home to well over 1,000 people. Many houses have vanished entirely, but many more remain, in varying states of decay. It is tempting to assume that it was the flooding of the lower valley that caused its depopulation, but as a matter of fact the story is considerably more complicated.

Growing Population

Settlement began in the area, previously a deer park, in the early part of the 16th century. The population grew over the next two centuries as woods were cleared. However, farming here was nearly always marginal. Most families supplemented their income by handloom weaving. Another widespread source of income was the distilling of illicit whisky. Many of the houses had secret passages or cellars to hide the stills.

As larger mills developed, handloom weaving became less viable. The construction of the Calf Hey Reservoir in the 1850s robbed the struggling community of its best land, but the final nail in the coffin was the crisis which afflicted agriculture in the 1880s, with drastic falls in commodity prices. There's an echo here of the problems which farmers are facing today. Once more, many farmers are searching for supplementary sources of income and in some cases leaving agriculture altogether.

Abandoned Farms

The crisis of the 1880s led to the abandonment of poorer upland farms in many parts of the region, but the total depopulation of the Grane Valley is one of the most dramatic instances. Even on the opening section of the walk, before crossing the main road, you pass the sites of several farms, a smithy and an inn – though all you're likely to see is a few remnants of wall incorporated into the boundary wall.

As the way swings round the head of the valley it passes several ruins. These stand around 1,000ft (305m) above sea level and it must always have been a somewhat bleak and exposed spot. It's hard to imagine these gaunt shells as they were, with adults working and perhaps children playing.

HASLINGDEN GRANE

Beyond the ruined farmsteads the walk route descends through a shady conifer plantation and then runs through broadleaved woods, notably a fine stand of beech. These plantings give some idea of how the valley might have looked before it was settled.

As you cross the dam of Calf Hey Reservoir, there are quarries on the skyline both ahead and behind, which also provided employment in the area. Walk 29 takes a closer look at the Musbury quarries. Just before the climb back to the road, the walk passes a graveyard and the sites of both the Methodist chapel and Anglican church. The latter has been re-erected lower down the valley, about 0.5 mile (800m) beyond the Duke of Wellington pub.

WALK 28 DIRECTIONS

❶ A footpath starts immediately left of the information centre. Go through a small plantation then climb alongside a wall. Go through a kissing gate by a Rossendale Way sign then go immediately left over a stone slab stile and follow an almost level path along a fine wall. After 100yds (91m) past a plantation, go left over a stile by a Rossendale Way sign and down to the road.

HASLINGDEN GRANE

❷ Go left down the road for 90yds (82m), then right on a track, swinging right to pass some ruins. After about 440yds (402m) the track swings left again near some spoil heaps. Stay on this past more ruins, then dip into a small valley alongside an old water-cut.

❸ At the end go right 50yds (46m) on a walled track, then left again across a short wet patch. Follow an old walled track past ruined houses and into another small valley, just above extensive ruins. Skirt rightwards round these and descend to the stream then climb up alongside a plantation. Cross into this at a kissing gate. The path starts level but soon begins to descend quite steeply, winding past Rossendale Way signs, to meet a clearer path at the bottom.

❹ Turn right, cross a footbridge and go up steps then across the hillside below a beech wood. Cross another small stream, go up a few paces then go left and follow a generally level path. Continue along a bilberry-covered hillside above Calf Hey Reservoir, passing a ruin on the left and through a dip containing a small stream. Another 90yds (82m) further, you'll see a large sycamore tree standing on its own.

❺ Go through a kissing gate just below the tree then descend slightly rightwards to a stile by the dam. Cross the dam and go up a tarmac path past some valve gear to reach a gate.

❻ Go through another gate on the right, then through a gap in the wall and up a path. This runs alongside the road to a car park. Where this path ends there's another up to the left, signed for Clough Head. Go up this, meeting the access road again, then continue up some steps and through a small plantation just below the main road. Go left up the road for 50yds (46m) then cross it by a footpath sign to a kissing gate opposite. A short footpath leads back to the start.

High on Hog Low Pike

With views over the Irwell, Darwen and Edgworth valleys.

See map and information panel for Walk 28

DISTANCE 6.75 miles (10.9km)   **MINIMUM TIME** 2hrs 30min

ASCENT/GRADIENT 820ft (250m) ▲▲▲   **LEVEL OF DIFFICULTY** +++

WALK 29 DIRECTIONS (Walk 28 option)

Just before the prominent sycamore at Point ❺ on Walk 28, another path goes sharply back right, signposted 'Edgworth'. Initially almost level, it climbs to cross the fence above the pine plantation. About 50yds (46m) further on, at a crossroads of faint paths, turn left and climb alongside the wire fence. Follow it above a steep slope to emerge on to wide moors.

The path forks by a marker post. Go right, across the dip, to a stile then follow the green path across the moor to Hog Low Pike (Point ❹). Though not quite the highest point on the walk, it is the most distinct summit.

Backtrack briefly then fork right. Follow a dilapidated wall and wire fence along the broad crest of the moor. The wall fades and the path shadows the fence, as it turns sharp right and over the slight rise of Causeway Height. Near a stile and gate go left on a green path across the moorland towards a stone wall. Follow it down left, cross at a gap and slant down to the ruins of Causeway End (Point ❸). From in front of the house angle down to a wall, parallel to the previous one.

At its end slant down to another ruin. Follow a narrow level path across the hillside to the ruins of Rushy Leach. Around 50yds (46m) further on, by the end of the wall, the path bears right. Follow it to a stile (Point ❸) near the corner of the next wall. Take a level green track, half left, through the old quarry workings and fork left after 50yds (46m).

When the chimney comes into view, go over the crossroads of routes, taking the narrow path slightly right, not the one directly ahead. Skirt the head of a steep 'canyon' and keep right to a stile in a fence. Descend over a second stile and steeply down to the bottom (Point ❹). Turn left on a wide, flagged track along the base of the steep slope to the inclined plane that runs down from the 'canyon'. Both were part of the tramway serving the quarries. There's a short tunnel through the incline, although officially the footpath goes round.

The path runs fairly level and then rises gently, below a steeper slope littered with waste stone. After crossing another stile you rejoin Walk 28 near the large sycamore (Point ❺).

Lever Park and Rivington Pike

A straightforward walk, though steep in places, taking in a superb viewpoint.

DISTANCE 3.75miles (6km) **MINIMUM TIME** 1hr 30min

ASCENT/GRADIENT 804ft (245m) ▲▲▲ **LEVEL OF DIFFICULTY** ✦✦✦

PATHS Mostly clear tracks, well-marked paths

LANDSCAPE Managed woodlands, rougher moors and formal gardens

SUGGESTED MAP OS Explorer 287 West Pennine Moors

START / FINISH Grid reference: SD 633145

DOG FRIENDLINESS Can mostly run free, but be careful crossing Rivington Lane and watch out for sheep on moors

PARKING At Hall Barn, in Lever Park

PUBLIC TOILETS Next to Great House Barn

WALK 30 DIRECTIONS

William Hesketh Lever, later Lord Leverhulme, left two great monuments in the region. One is Port Sunlight (see Walk 6). The other is Lever Park, which he bought in 1900. Born in Bolton, Lever made a fortune from soap, and spent much of it on philanthropic projects. He intended to present the park to the people of Bolton but legal wranglings resulted in it being gifted to Liverpool instead, though it's the inhabitants of Bolton and Chorley who get the benefit. It can get very busy.

Go round the right side of Hall Barn to a red-brick house then down the drive, between ponds, and on down an avenue of beech trees. Keep straight on and cross the busy road to Great House Barn. Walk down the track away from it, towards the lake, then go left by some iron railings. Skirt the conservation area and wind round to the lakeshore. Keep to the lower path, which leads

to The Castle. This is a replica of Liverpool Castle, not as it appeared in its heyday but in the dilapidated condition in which it appeared around 1900. On Walk 15 you can see where the castle once actually stood.

From the castle gate take the long track running straight away. Just before a barrier, with a car park beyond, go left on a short track to the road then straight up the track opposite. This track can sometimes be a bit muddy, but climbs steadily up the left side of a wood before angling left to join a wide gravel track.

In just a few paces, go sharply back right on a path below a gorse-covered slope. This meets a stony track. Go left through the gate and up the track. Keep on climbing steadily as the gorse thins out and the track doubles back right near a gate (this leads into the Terraced Gardens). The tower on the summit of Rivington Pike soon appears, a lot closer now than it was before.

Go through a gate and you'll see that rough paths climb up left directly towards the tower, but it's a lot less steep to stick to the track then go right at the junction by a prominent signpost where the mast on Winter Hill also comes into view. Go slightly downhill to a gated track on the left. Climb this wide, stony route through a couple of curves then finish straight up on steep and eroded paths to the tower.

Rivington Pike is 1,198ft (365m) high and was a beacon site known to have been used to warn of the arrival of the Spanish Armada. The tower was built in 1733. It gives a tremendous view over most of Lancashire, extending to Cheshire, Wales and the Lake District. At closer quarters two prominent features are the Reebok Stadium, home of Bolton Wanderers, and the long brick sheds of the Horwich locomotive works.

Descend the stone steps in front of the tower then more steps cutting the corner of the track. Then join the track, almost level now, to a gate just a small building. Go right on a wide and fenced track, to the tall, narrow Pigeon Tower. From this, backtrack for about 100yds (91m) to a fork and take the lower track between some stone gateposts. This leads into the Terraced Gardens. You can wander and explore pleasantly here for hours and the described route is just one suggestion.

The track leads to a broad level space with the remains of a tile floor, site of a substantial bungalow. Just beyond this, go down steps to a flagged path. Where it splits go left and down more steps and out on to a balcony. Go down and left along the track below, then right through a small arch and down more steps.

Cross a rough track and continue down beside some ruins. Curl down below them and there's a pool on the left, complete with waterfall and grotto. Turn right before a rough stone arch and cross a wider path to descend a narrower one slanting to the right. Keep descending in the same general direction, at the same easy gradient, until the track swings left as the slope begins to ease.

Go straight down across a field then through a gate into woodland again. Keep straight on then swing right on a track flanked by a wooden fence. Go through the gate and continue straight ahead, with some buildings on your left, back to the car park.

Darwen Tower and the Freedom of the Moors

A simple walk, if moderately steep in parts, to a great physical and historical landmark on the moors.

DISTANCE *4 miles (6.4km)* MINIMUM TIME *1hr 30min*
ASCENT/GRADIENT *705ft (215m)* ▲▲▲ LEVEL OF DIFFICULTY +++
PATHS *Well-defined tracks throughout, 1 stile*
LANDSCAPE *Reservoir and wooded surroundings, farmland, open moors*
SUGGESTED MAP *OS Explorer 287 West Pennine Moors*
START / FINISH *Grid reference: SD 665215*
DOG FRIENDLINESS *Dogs can run free on tracks, watch for sheep on moor*
PARKING *Pay car park near Royal Arms*
PUBLIC TOILETS *At car park*

The 'right to roam' may be still in the process of being established over most of England and Wales, but has been enjoyed on the Darwen Moors for more than a century, and Darwen Tower stands in commemoration. After a long struggle, spearheaded by the Ashton family, rights of access over the moors were transferred to Darwen Corporation in 1896. A large procession of local people climbed on to the moor in celebration.

It is worth remembering that in this, as in most other cases, what was really happening was the re-establishment of rights of access that had existed for centuries. Local people would cross the moors on their way to work in the mills and in the small collieries that existed here. The erosion of these rights in favour of 'sporting' interests caused much resentment and was not forgotten. Free access to these moors today is a right, but should also be considered both a privilege and a responsibility.

Pleasant Stages

The opening stages of the walk are a pleasant preamble, through the shady woods around Upper Roddlesworth Reservoir and over a shoulder by some old tracks to Earnsdale Reservoir. Here you are just above Sunnyhurst Wood, Darwen's main park, which provide a direct link from the town on to the wilderness of the moors. Above the reservoirs you climb in stages. After the old quarry you begin the final, longest stage, on a corner of the moors overlooking the town.

India Mill and Darwen Tower

The dominant features, without question, are the India Mill and Darwen Tower. The India Mill dates from the 1860s; the chimney is 302ft (92m) high and its style is not Indian but Italianate. The mill closed in 1991 but now houses new light industry and office space, with a range of retail and leisure developments in the subsidiary buildings.

Construction began on the Darwen Tower in 1897, the year after the achievement of access, which also happened to be the Diamond Jubilee of Queen Victoria. The building was opened in 1898. There are 65 wide stone steps, and then 16 iron ones leading to the small glasshouse on the top. The tower did fall into some decay during the middle of the 20th century but was thoroughly restored, with funds from a public appeal, in the 1970s.

Naturally the view is extensive, especially in the northern half. Some of it has changed totally since the tower was built; the new industrial areas alongside the M65 above Blackburn are the most obvious example. But the skylines of Bowland and Pendle are the same. The descent takes you past some old mine workings and a waterworks channel. Just before the end, the row of houses (Hollinshead Terrace) was built as workers' accommodation for a nearby mill that no longer exists.

WALK 31 DIRECTIONS

❶ From the car park cross a bus turning area and then the road for a signposted public footpath around wooden barriers. In a few paces go right, following the sign 'Woods and Water Trail'. The path descends steadily to a crossroads. Turn right here on a broad path – still the 'Woods and Water Trail' – then after 200yds (183m) go right at a fork on a gently rising path. Gradually curve to the right and climb a little more steeply, with open fields on the left, out to the road. Go left for 200yds (183m).

❷ Go right up a walled track on the far side of Fine Peters Farm.

Go straight on at a junction then descend steeply, with a section of old paving, towards Earnsdale Reservoir. Cross the dam and swing left at its end then follow the lane up right until it swings left once more, over a cattle grid. Go straight up the steep grass slope ahead, skirting a fenced area with regenerating trees.

tower comes into view bear right, past a marker stone on which there is a likeness of the tower, and straight up to the real thing.

❹ From the tower bear left past the trig point and then along a broad path above the steeper slope that falls to Sunnyhurst Hey Reservoir. Where the path swings left, by the second bench, take the second path on the right, overlooking the valley of Stepback Brook and go down a zig-zag path. Don't cross the stile ahead but go back left, and finally over a stile at the bottom. Go left on a track to cross the stream.

❸ Go left on a track then, just above Water House, bear right to walk up a concrete track. At a gap in the aluminium barrier bear left on a level path to reach an old quarry. Once there, go up right on a stony track then, above the sign, keep left where it forks. A gate on the left gives a good view of the town of Darwen, dominated by the India Mill chimney. Continue up the main track for another 100yds (91m). As the gradient eases and the

❺ The track swings back right and up through a wood. As it levels out pass to the right of a pair of gates and continue down towards a row of houses. A lane just left of these leads to the road. Go back past the bus turning area to the car park.

Weaving Ways Around Wycoller and Trawden

A moderate walk around an upland district steeped in the history of Lancashire, Yorkshire and the textile industry.

DISTANCE 5.25 miles (8.4km)   **MINIMUM TIME** 2hrs

ASCENT/GRADIENT 538ft (164m) ▲▲▲   **LEVEL OF DIFFICULTY** ✦✦✦

PATHS Field paths, some rough tracks and quiet lanes, 19 stiles

LANDSCAPE Upland pastures, moorland and wooded valley

SUGGESTED MAP OS Explorer OL21 South Pennines

START / FINISH Grid reference: SD 926395

DOG FRIENDLINESS Under control around livestock and on Access Land, where you must keep to the public right of way between points ❺ and ❻

PARKING Car park just above Wycoller village

PUBLIC TOILETS In Wycoller village

Everyone associates the Brontës with Yorkshire, but they had strong Lancashire connections too. As children the sisters lived in the north of the county, attending school at Cowan Bridge, only later moving to Haworth, where they wrote their famous books. Haworth is only 9 miles (14.5km) from Wycoller and today you step out on a small section of the waymarked Brontë Way.

Handloom Weavers

Another hint of Yorkshire is the tradition of weaving wool, rather than the cotton usually associated with Lancashire. Trawden had several mills. Wycoller was a community of handloom weavers but as the Industrial Revolution developed they were unable to compete with the growth of larger, powered mills and the village became an isolated backwater.

Sheep and Cattle

Naturally sheep farming is important here, especially on the higher ground, but the area has a long tradition of cattle rearing too. The distinctive walls of large upright slabs that are seen in places are known as vaccary walls – a vaccary being a cattle farm.

Quiet First Half

The first half of the walk crosses these pastures, though you will see more sheep grazing than cattle today. For much of the way you climb gently, with wide views towards Pendle and the Yorkshire Dales, finally emerging on to the open moors. The route now follows an old trackway along the edge of the moor before swinging back down into Turnhole Clough. The path skirts above the woods before dropping into them and crossing the beck. Just below you meet the main Wycoller Beck. About 300yds (274m) below the confluence is the Clam Bridge, believed to be more than 1,000 years old and made of a single massive slab of gritstone. At least, it was a single slab until 1989, when an exceptionally heavy flood swept the bridge away.

It was repaired and replaced, but damaged again the following year. Though the repair has been skilfully done, you can clearly see where the slab was broken by the torrent of water.

Wycoller Hamlet

Following the stream, you soon come into Wycoller hamlet. Despite its simple construction of stone slabs, the clapper bridge is a relatively recent affair, at most only 200 years old. The packhorse bridge is certainly more ancient, possibly over 700 years old. The low parapets, which sometimes alarm nervous parents (though usually not their children), are an essential feature for a packhorse bridge as the animals would be heavily burdened with huge bales of wool.

Broken Up

Near by stand the ruins of Wycoller Hall. Originally built in the 16th century, the Hall was considerably enlarged in the 18th century by Henry Cunliffe. Unfortunately the lavish works left him heavily in debt and after his death, in 1818, the estate was broken up. It's thought that the Hall was largely derelict by the time the Brontë sisters knew about it and that it inspired Ferndean Manor in Charlotte's *Jane Eyre* (1847).

WYCOLLER

WALK 32 DIRECTIONS

1 At the top of the car park are a noticeboard and beyond this a sign 'Wycoller 500m'. Follow the footpath indicated, just above the road, until it joins it on a bend. Cross the first of two stiles on the right and slant right across the field to another stile, then up to a gate and into a garden. Follow the arrow through trees up the left side to another stile.

2 Bear right, past Bracken Hill house, then go left to cross a stream, up towards a house on the skyline, until a footbridge and stile appear in a dip. Follow the hedge and then a wall in the same line. When it ends at open, rushy pasture bear slightly right (towards Pendle Hill, if clear). Cresting the rise, you'll see a stile and signpost by a corner of walls. The sign for Trawden points too far right. Aim slightly left, between two power line poles and again, once over a rise, you'll see a stile and signpost by the end of a fine wall. Follow the wall and then a walled track to Higher Stunstead. Go past the first buildings and into the yard.

3 Go left up a walled track to a cattle grid then keep ahead to reach a stile and alongside a stream up to Little Laith. Go past the house on your left then go right, through the second gate, along field-edges, to a large barn on the skyline by New Laith. Follow arrows round the farm.

4 Continue straight ahead to a stile by a gate and over more stiles to Mean Moss. Go a few paces left up a track then follow the wall on the right and more stiles to Beaver. Go slightly right down a field to a stile near the corner then up by the stream to a track.

5 Go left, then keep straight on by the wall following a rougher track (Pendle Way sign). When the wall turns sharp left, the track bends gradually, above a stream.

6 At the Access Land notice go slightly left to a stile by a gate then take the lower path, down towards the stream then up round a wood. From a kissing gate drop down to cross the stream, then follow it down and out to a lane.

7 Go left down the lane to the visitor centre and Wycoller hamlet. From here, continue along the lane and join the outward part of the route for the last 350yds (320m) back to the car park.

Witching Ways
of Pendle

A grand loop around the flanks and subsidiary
ridges of Pendle Hill.

DISTANCE 4.75 miles (7.7km)   **MINIMUM TIME** 2hrs

ASCENT/GRADIENT 738ft (225m) ▲▲▲   **LEVEL OF DIFFICULTY** +++

PATHS *Field paths and rough moorland, surfaced track, 11 stiles*

LANDSCAPE *Wooded foothills and moorland slopes*

SUGGESTED MAP *OS Explorer OL21 South Pennines;*
Explorer OL41 Forest of Bowland & Ribblesdale

START / FINISH *Grid reference: SD 823403*

DOG FRIENDLINESS *Can run free in woodland and enclosed tracks*

PARKING *Public pay car park in Barley village*

PUBLIC TOILETS *At car park and at Newchurch in Pendle*

The name Pendle Hill means 'Hill Hill Hill'. The way this came about is typical of the convoluted history behind so many English place names. If you lived below Pendle, you might well call it simply 'the Hill', and early Celtic inhabitants did just that – 'Pen'. Later incomers, not realising this, called it Pendle, meaning 'the hill called Pen'. This meaning too became obscured, and the name was later applied to the whole district.

The Wild High Moors

Pendle is also associated with witches. In 1612 seven women and two men were hanged at Lancaster Castle (see Walk 50). Another old woman died in prison before the case was even tried. Several of the accused confessed, but whether any of them were witches is an almost unanswerable question. The story is well told in several books, notably Robert Neill's classic novel, *Mist Over Pendle* (1951), it remains in print and is readily available in the area.

The walk starts easily, on a well-marked and much-trodden route (part of the Pendle Way) through green fields. While this shorter loop avoids the challenge of the steep upper slopes, it does make a fairly level, but moderately rough, traverse along their base, giving a taste of the wilder atmosphere of the high moors. Perhaps you can begin to appreciate how isolated and remote parts of the district may have felt in the 17th century.

Alice Nutter

From the plantations and reservoirs of Ogden Clough climb on to a subsidiary ridge for the best views of the walk, then descend to the small village of Newchurch in Pendle. It was new in 1544, anyway! Although no one knows for sure, it is thought that Malkin Tower, where the witches met, was situated near by. On the tower of St Mary's Church is the 'Eye of God', which was supposed to protect the villagers from witchcraft, and in the churchyard there's a 'witch's grave', possibly that of Alice Nutter.

Beyond Newchurch the route follows the ridge, looking down on Roughlee, though caravan sites make it hard to visualise the 17th-century landscape. Roughlee was the home of Alice Nutter, a gentlewoman who was among those hanged at Lancaster. Although poor, old women, especially widows, were most likely to be suspect, no one was exempt from the paranoia of the times. Anyone who kept a dog or cat, for instance, ran the risk of being accused of consorting with a 'familiar spirit'.

WALK 33 DIRECTIONS

❶ From the toilets follow a path rightwards across the green then over a footbridge. Go right up the

street. Just past Meadow Bank Farm turn left alongside a stream.

❷ Keep straight on up then cross another footbridge and join a lane. Go left and follow this clear and well-signposted route past a building then up to Brown House. Go into the yard, right on a track for 60yds (55m) then left through another kissing gate. Follow the obvious path through a small hollow with newly planted trees and straight up to a gate left of Pendle House.

3 Go left to meet a path just above the wall. After another gate, climb a little, away from the wall. The path runs an undulating course, then dips more definitely and meets the wall again. From a stile (don't cross it) just above Under Pendle, bear right and

follow the fence. Cross the stream then straight on up a clearer track to rejoin the wall.

4 Bear right on a trackway climbing alongside an obvious groove. Beyond a couple of old wooden gateposts, go left through the 5-bar gate (not the kissing gate) and straight downhill with the wall on your left. Cross a track and descend steeply to a gate just below Upper Ogden Reservoir.

5 Follow the reservoir road until just above Lower Ogden Reservoir. Go right over a bridge, down a few steps then round right to a footbridge. Climb some steps and then go left to climb more steps through a plantation. At its end go up right to the ridge.

6 Turn left following a fence then a wall. Beyond a wall gate veer right, keeping roughly level until the rooftops of Newchurch appear. Aim for a water trough, then a stile and signpost. Descend a short path to the road.

7 Go down the road opposite, called Jinny Lane. After about 100yds (91m) cross a stile on the left-hand side and follow a rising footpath. Fork to the left just inside a plantation. At the far end of the plantation keep straight on, gradually converging with the wall on the left-hand side. Follow the wall, changing sides half-way along, to join a sunken track. Cross this and descend to reach the road.

8 Go down the tarmac track opposite, cross the Pendle Water then go left alongside it. Continue on a stonier track past some cottages and a converted mill. Finally a short path on the right leads back to the car park.

The Big End of Pendle Hill

An extended loop and a steep climb to Lancashire's most celebrated summit.

See map and information panel for Walk 33

| DISTANCE 6 miles (9.7km) | MINIMUM TIME 3hrs |
| ASCENT/GRADIENT 1,427ft (435m) ▲▲▲ | LEVEL OF DIFFICULTY +++ |

WALK 34 DIRECTIONS
(Walk 33 option)

Pendle Hill is not the highest hill in Lancashire, but it is the best known, most recognisable and surely the best loved, which ultimately counts for more than mere height. Along with witches, it has more salubrious associations. It was on Pendle that George Fox had a life-changing vision that inspired the birth of the Society of Friends (the Quakers).

From the gate by Pendle House (Point ❸) bear right and up to a kissing gate. Climb straight up on a remade path that soon swings right above the very steep slope by a staircase of large blocks. George Fox 'went on the top of it with much ado, it was so steep,' and you will surely sympathise. As the gradient eases there's a wall and a marker post. Go left before the wall, joining a well-worn track to the trig point, standing on a hump (Point ❹), that may be a Bronze-Age burial mound.

The top is a sprawling plateau, which restricts the views westward, but the eastern half is great. The valley of Pendle Water is directly below. The Yorkshire boundary – and the Pennine Way – run across the first range of hills to the east. Further north

is a green expanse, crossed by the Ribble and Aire, and then the Yorkshire Dales National Park. South are Colne, Nelson and Burnley and then more hills, half in Yorkshire, half in Lancashire.

Continue in the same direction, past a huge untidy cairn. At a second enormous cairn the path splits. Keep right past occasional smaller cairns, until the grassy but wide and recognisable path splits again. Take the right branch, which swings further right then runs down past widely-spaced cairns and meets a tiny stream. This soon grows and carves itself a more distinct valley, Boar Clough. Cross the stream but keep following it down into Ogden Clough.

The descent gets very steep just before the end. Keep right, where it's a little less steep, then go left on a relatively level path. Ford the beck (Point ❸) and go up a little. Contour along the slope then go roughly down to a gate. Follow a narrow clear path above Upper Ogden Reservoir, crossing the wall half-way along at a gate. Descend by the dam, joining the reservoir road. Walk 33 comes down from the left just here (Point ❺).

Rural Revelations in Witton

Not just a country park but real countryside in the heart of urban Lancashire.

DISTANCE 4.5 miles (7.2km)	MINIMUM TIME 1hr 30min
ASCENT/GRADIENT 558ft (170m) ▲▲▲	LEVEL OF DIFFICULTY +++

PATHS Good paths and tracks, some open fields, 6 stiles

LANDSCAPE Woodland, pasture and river bank

SUGGESTED MAP OS Explorer 287 West Pennine Moors

START / FINISH Grid reference: SD 663271

DOG FRIENDLINESS Can run free in country park, but on lead on farmland

PARKING Large car park just off A674

PUBLIC TOILETS Adjacent to The Pavilion and at visitor centre

WALK 35 DIRECTIONS

Glance at the map and you may think this is an urban walk, but that's not how it feels. The urban backdrop is mostly unseen, though it may come to your ears over the birdsong in Billinge Wood.

Witton Country Park covers 480 acres (194ha) and was formerly the estate surrounding Witton House. The house was demolished though the stable block is now a visitor centre. The park has a network of nature trails, but the walk ventures into open country.

Walk past the athletics track and The Pavilion in the park, then go left, below the woods, following

WHAT TO LOOK OUT FOR

Specimen trees abound on the wooded slopes of Billinge Hill, many still bearing identifying signs, albeit a little faded. Keep an eye out for the the nuthatch, sparrow-sized but with a slaty-blue back, which clings to the bark of the trees.

the cycle track until it swings left. There's a sculpture, 'Snowy the Crow', perched on a tree on the right. Just before this there are two tracks on the right. Take the left one, a public bridleway, by a sign for 'Crow Wood'.

Follow the track up through a wooded dell. Cross a small bridge over a side stream then go up some steps. Go left at the top of these then round to the right, climbing an ever-narrower belt of woodland and via two sets of kissing gates.

At the top, near Billinge Nook farm, go a few paces right on the lane then through a short tunnel and up the track rising to the right, past some magnificent beech trees. Cross one path on a counter-diagonal and continue until ours doubles back, by a wooden post bearing a blue public bridleway arrow.

As the gradient eases, birch and scattered pine rise above the rhododendrons. Stick to the principal path and you soon reach a small open area with a concrete plinth and plaque. This is the summit of Billinge Hill. The views are limited to strategic gaps in the trees: south to Darwen Tower and Winter Hill, east to Blackburn cathedral and Pendle Hill, north to Mellor and the Bowland Fells.

Continue beyond the summit, swing left, then go left on a broad,

---

WHERE TO EAT AND DRINK

The Old Stables Tearoom at Witton Park visitor centre is open from 1pm to 4.30pm, opening at 11am on Sundays and bank holidays. For pub food try the Clog and Billycock on Billinge End Road – a billycock is an old name for a bowler hat.

---

straight track. Ignore all paths off, including the waymarked public bridleway down to the right, and descend down the steepening hillside to a T-junction with another path. Go right, initially uphill, before swinging back left to a small parking area. At one corner of this, where wall meets fence, is a stile and a Witton Weavers' Way sign.

Go straight across the field, a little right of the crest, to a stile by a small clump of trees (there are larger patches of trees to the left and to right). Just ahead is a knoll above a small old quarry; this is a much better viewpoint than Billinge Hill. The area is known locally as Yellow Hills because of the stands of bright yellow gorse.

Carry on down a rough spine, passing walls of single upright stones. Hoghton Tower on its wooded hill is dead ahead. Go downhill and over stiles in the bottom left corner, into the woods shielding the depths of Butler

Delf, an old quarry (the Butler family owned Pleasington Hall).

Near some houses go left a few paces on the track that leads into the quarry, then right at a public footpath sign. Follow this path down and keep straight on, by an old wall in the trees on your left, over a stile into open fields. Keep straight on in the same line, passing midway between two power line poles, then down to the right edge of the wood ahead.

In the bottom right corner, just right of Pleasington Old Hall, there's a stile and 30yds (27m) beyond it a drive. Go right for 200yds (183m) then left along the cycle track, past an ornate milepost. Go past a pool with a view of Pleasington Old Hall,

---

WHILE YOU'RE THERE

Hoghton Tower, glimpsed during the walk, is a late 16th-century house with a hilltop setting, open to the public in the summer. Legend states that it was in the banqueting hall, that James I 'knighted' a fine joint of beef, giving rise to the name 'sirloin'.

---

then right down the drive below the cemetery. The gates may be locked to vehicles but pedestrians can still get through. Bear left across sports pitches to a metal footbridge, cross it then go left just above the river, dropping down further on to follow the bank through woods.

The next bridge has decorated 'gateposts' and another fancy milepost further on. The mileposts are two of 1,000 placed on the National Cycle Network during Millennium year. Cross this bridge then continue along the river bank and so back to the start.

Round the Hodder Valley

A straightforward walk around the delightful heart of the Forest of Bowland.

DISTANCE 7 miles (11.3km)   **MINIMUM TIME** 2hrs 30min

ASCENT/GRADIENT 853ft (260m) ▲▲▲   **LEVEL OF DIFFICULTY** ✦✦✦

PATHS Field paths, farm tracks and quiet lane, 12 stiles

LANDSCAPE Pasture and river valley, overlooked by high bare hills

SUGGESTED MAP OS Explorer OL41 Forest of Bowland & Ribblesdale

START / FINISH Grid reference: SD 658468

DOG FRIENDLINESS Grazing land, keep dogs on leads

PARKING Roadside parking near Inn at Whitewell or below church

PUBLIC TOILETS At Dunsop Bridge (see Walk 37)

With two sets of stepping stones to cross, this walk could be problematic when the river is in flood – but the good thing is that you will know immediately if this is so. Should this be the case you'll then have the choice of moving elsewhere or simply drowning your sorrows at The Inn at Whitewell.

Limestone Quarries

Having crossed the river, you climb around the flanks of New Laund Hill and then cross another small ridge into the valley of Dinkling Green Brook. There are several exposures of limestone, mostly the result of quarrying, on the ridge just north of the track. Limestone, which underlies most of the ground covered by the walk, tends to produce good grazing conditions, unlike the more acid soils formed on the gritstone of the higher fells.

As the 'Forest' element in 'Forest of Bowland' suggests, the area was once dominated by hunting, especially of deer. (The name 'laund', as in New Laund, means a hunting park.) 'Forest' does not automatically imply tree-cover, as it does to us today, but the valleys and lower slopes certainly were much more wooded. By the later Middle Ages, however, there was a shift towards farming and trees were cleared to be replaced by pasture for both sheep and cattle.

An Ancient Ford

Knot Hill Quarry is the largest exposure of limestone on the walk, and marks the start of the descent back towards the second crossing of the Hodder. This is another grand line of stepping stones alongside an ancient ford. Stepping stones are fine for us, after all, but they are of little use to livestock. In medieval times bridging a river like the Hodder was a major undertaking and fords were therefore of great significance. It's no surprise, then, to find another substantial farm immediately beyond the crossing. Stakes is a particularly fine 17th-century farmhouse.

After Stakes the route rises away from the river, but dips back towards it before climbing in earnest. Above a plantation you cross a large open field which has been created from several smaller ones: the faint ridges and furrows of the old field boundaries can still be seen and initially the path follows one of them. Beyond this there's a little more climbing before a green path contours above the valley, giving a great view of the ground you've covered and then, as it swings around, over Whitewell towards Dunsop Bridge and the wilder country beyond.

The final descent takes you past the burial ground. Its separation from the church may strike you as odd – though in many parts of the world this is normal practice. Here it probably results from the limited space around the church and the potential danger of flooding on the ground below it.

WALK 36 DIRECTIONS

1 From the lower parking area follow the river bank left to the stepping stones. Climb just right of the woods and through the farmyard of New Laund. By an old cheese press go left on a curving track below slopes, then up a field. Bear left to a gate on to a lane. Go a few paces left to a stile on the right.

> ### WHAT TO LOOK OUT FOR
> Just below Knot Hill Quarry there's a good example of a lime kiln. By heating the crushed stone carbon dioxide was driven off leaving fairly pure calcium (lime). This was used for fertiliser, mortar and whitewash. There are fossil-rich blocks in some of the walls, notably on the high path before the final descent.

2 Cross rough pasture, aiming just left of the house, then go right on the surfaced track, swinging round into another little valley. Go left to a farm, then right, through the farmyard to a footbridge.

3 Turn left, past chicken coops, to a stile on the right. Cross a field corner to another stile then go straight on to Dinkling Green Farm. A gap to the right of the cow shed leads into the farmyard.

4 Half-way down the yard go right, between buildings, to a

> ### WHILE YOU'RE THERE
> The Bowland Wild Boar Park lies within the loop of the walk. As well as wild boars, it also has deer, llamas and a variety of smaller animals. Browsholme Hall has been in the same family for 600 years, though the building 'only' dates back to 1507.

> ### WHERE TO EAT AND DRINK
> The Inn at Whitewell is enormously popular but there's plenty of room. The main bar is usually busy yet relaxed, there's good beer and food.

ford. Keep left past a plantation, follow the next right-hand field-edge then go through a gate in a dip. Follow the hedge round then cross it via a gate and over a rise. Bear right, down to the beck, then up the lane to Lickhurst Farm.

5 Turn left into the farmyard then bear right and straight on down a track. When it swings right, go left before the next gate then straight ahead on an intermittent track.

6 Just before Knot Hill Quarry, turn left, past a lime kiln, to a junction. Go right and down to a lane. Go left then left again, round a bend and down. Cross a bridge on the right and head right towards Stakes farm, crossing the river on more stepping stones.

7 Turn left and climb above the river. At the next junction go over a stile and turn left, descend steeply, then swing right, slightly above the River Hodder, to a stile. Beyond a ford go up a faint track and keep climbing past the right edge of a plantation. Keep straight on across an open field to a stile in the furthest corner.

8 Turn left then go through an iron gate on the right. Bear left and contour round the hill, just above the fence, to more gates. After 100yds (91m) go left down through an aluminium gate. The track swings right. Just past Seed Hill Cottage turn left and descend steps by the burial ground. A short steep lane descends to the start.

Right: Forest of Bowland at Whitewell (Walk 36)

Moors at the Centre

*A tough walk that gives walkers the
chance to taste the exhilarating
freedom of the high moors.*

DISTANCE 9.25 miles (14.9km)   MINIMUM TIME 3hrs 30min
ASCENT/GRADIENT 1,247ft (380m) ▲▲▲   LEVEL OF DIFFICULTY +++
PATHS Field paths, rougher moorland paths, surfaced road, 10 stiles
LANDSCAPE Rough pasture, exposed moorland, sheltered valley
SUGGESTED MAP OS Explorer OL41 Forest of Bowland & Ribblesdale
START / FINISH Grid reference: SD 662501
DOG FRIENDLINESS Access Land, keep dogs on lead
PARKING Public car park at Dunsop Bridge
PUBLIC TOILETS At car park

There aren't many places where a phone box is a tourist attraction, but the one at Dunsop Bridge is deemed to stand at the centre point of Great Britain. This apart, Dunsop Bridge lacks amusements for less energetic visitors, but it lacks nothing for magnificent surroundings and is the starting point for many great walks. This route uses something which is quite a rarity in Bowland, a public footpath crossing the tops.

To reach it you cross a stretch of upland pasture. This gives easy walking, rarely steep, except where it dips into Oxenhurst Clough. The clough frames a view of the small conical hill called Knot or Sugar Loaf, which began as a coral reef 250 million years ago. The ascent to the plateau is by a well-defined ridge, giving wider views than from the level top. The prospect takes in the Hodder Valley, Stocks Reservoir and Gisburn Forest, the broader sweep of Ribblesdale and the Yorkshire hills.

Heather Moors
The heather moors of Bowland have traditionally been managed for grouse shooting. In recent years, for reasons that are not fully understood, grouse numbers have declined substantially. This has affected the livelihood of many local people and has had a knock-on effect on other species. Hen harriers, for instance, prey in part on grouse chicks.

The Birds of Bowland Project
In the past walkers, conservationists and shooting interests have sometimes viewed each other suspiciously. Gamekeepers have been accused of poisoning birds of prey. Today, however, there is a new spirit of co-operation. The Birds of Bowland Project involves the RSPB, United Utilities (a major landowner) and receives funding from the Heritage Lottery Fund and Ribble Valley District Council. The aim is to encourage sympathetic management of the distinctive habitat and to protect the bird populations. One result should be to encourage more visitors to the area, something which has been further helped by recess Access legislation, granting wider access to open country.

DUNSOP BRIDGE

The moorland crossing is all too brief before the descent into Whitendale. Here there are reminders that Bowland is a significant water catchment. The track you join near Whitendale Farm is the line of a water pipe. The main waterworks intake is a little further down the valley and from here you follow the access road most of the way back to Dunsop Bridge.

WALK 37 DIRECTIONS

1 From the public car park in Dunsop Bridge, go up a surfaced track, passing just to the left of the local post office and tea room,

for about 800yds (732m). When you reach the end of the track, by some houses, follow a public footpath ahead for another 100yds (91m) and then turn right, up a steep bank.

2 Cross the large field, bearing slightly left to meet power lines. Continue to a stile just before Beatrix farm. Follow the track to just before the second set of buildings. Go left, through the second of two gates. Climb the slope right of a small stream, over a stile, then follow a wire fence across the hillside. Drop into Oxenhurst Clough then climb out through a plantation, rejoining the fence as the gradient eases. Keep straight on to join another track.

3 Go left and follow the track for 0.75 mile (1.2km) to Burn House, where it swings right. Bear away left, slanting down and across an open field, towards the middle of a young plantation. Follow the path through it, bearing right to a stile. Aim just right of another young plantation in a dip, then cross a field towards a house (Laythams). Go left on the lane for 300yds (274m).

4 Turn left up a metalled track. Clearly marked gates guide you round Burnside Cottage. About 50yds (46m) above this, drop to the stream and continue up to its left. From the top of the enclosure a path rises to the right alongside an obvious groove, then swings back left. Climb steadily up a ridge and then swing rightwards above the upper reaches of

Dunsop Brook. Cross a broad plateau, roughly parallel to an old wall, to a circular patch of stones.

5 Turn left and cross the wall at a gate. The path beyond is rough but clear. After a slight rise it descends, gently at first but gradually getting steeper. As the ground really steepens, descend in big zig-zags, with a gate half-way down. Just above the farm at Whitendale go left beside a wall.

6 Follow a conspicuously level track for 0.75 mile (1.2km) until it swings round a little side valley, over two footbridges. Cross a stile and wind down to a track by the river. Follow this down to a bridge by some waterworks.

7 Cross the bridge, join the road and follow it steadily down the valley for 1.5 miles (2.4km), past Bishop's House.

8 After a cattle grid, cross the river on a substantial footbridge. Just beyond this you rejoin the outward route.

Left: Forest of Bowland at Slaidburn (Walk 37)

Hurst Green and Three Rivers

Did these rivers, fields and woods inspire Tolkien's fantastical creation of The Shire?

DISTANCE 6.5 miles (10.4km)   MINIMUM TIME 2hrs

ASCENT/GRADIENT 459ft (140m) ▲▲▲   LEVEL OF DIFFICULTY ✦✦✦

PATHS Grassy riverside paths, woodland and farm tracks, 11 stiles

LANDSCAPE Pastoral scenery, scattered woodlands, backdrop of moors

SUGGESTED MAP OS Explorer 287 West Pennine Moors

START / FINISH Grid reference: SD 684382

DOG FRIENDLINESS Can run free in woodland sections

PARKING By Hurst Green village hall or on roadside adjacent

PUBLIC TOILETS Centre of Hurst Green

Y ou don't have to be a Tolkien fan to enjoy this walk, which has long been recognised as a logical and graceful outing.

Tolkien Connection

Recent research by Jonathan Hewat (a teacher at Stonyhurst's prep school, St Mary's Hall) has uncovered the extent of the Tolkien connection. This much is certain: J R R Tolkien, author of *The Lord of the Rings*, knew this area well. One of his sons studied for the priesthood at Stonyhurst and Tolkien spent long periods here while he was writing the trilogy. The rest, though fascinating, is largely conjecture. In the hobbits' Shire there's a River Shirebourn, and the Shireburn family once owned Stonyhurst. But does that mean that Hurst Green is Hobbiton?

Tolkien also drew great inspiration from the country of his boyhood in the West Midlands, deeply regretting its disappearance under roads and factories. Perhaps the enduringly green Ribble Valley reminded him of that lost landscape. No doubt The Shire owes something to both. If the Tolkien angle intrigues you, a locally available leaflet gives much more detail.

Just after the Ribble, you pass the aqueduct, built in 1880 to supply water to Blackburn. An easy 0.75 mile (1.2km) brings you to Jumbles Rocks, outcrops of limestone which form natural weirs and a ford. The ford has been used, when the water's low, since time immemorial. Until the 1950s there was a ferry and the Boat House was the ferryman's home.

In the fields near by are two mounds. The lower one was excavated in 1894 and dated to *c*1250 BC. The larger, though known to be artificial, has yet to be properly examined. As the Ribble swings round, the River Calder enters opposite, close to 17th-century Hacking Hall. Less than 0.75 mile (1.2km) further on is the confluence of the Ribble and the Hodder, which you follow briefly before leaving it near Winkley Hall.

You'll soon return to the river at Low Hodder Bridge. Just downstream is the ancient Cromwell's Bridge – a misnomer. The bridge was built for one of the Shireburn dynasty in 1562. Legend has it that Cromwell vandalised it, destroying the parapets that impeded the progress of his troops.

HURST GREEN

You follow the Hodder for almost another mile (1.6km) before climbing steeply away to Woodfields. Tolkien stayed in one of these houses. The track passes St Mary's Hall and then reaches Hall Barn Farm. Nearby, on the edge of the college precincts is a small observatory. This was one of a network, observations from which helped the Norwegian physicist Kristian Birkeland confirm the magnetic origin of the Northern Lights.

WALK 38 DIRECTIONS

❶ Walk down the road to reach the centre of Hurst Green village. Cross the main road and go down left of The Shireburn pub to a stile below the main car park.

Go down the edge of a field and then follow a small stream to reach some duckboards and a footbridge. After a slight rise, descend via a stile and winding path to the River Ribble. Bear left just above the river.

WALK 38

2 Skirt the aqueduct and return to the river bank. Join a surfaced drive past Jumbles Rocks. Go over a large wooden stile beyond a small stone building to rejoin the river bank and follow it, towards the Boat House.

3 After rounding the big bend, go up slightly to a track. Follow this for about 0.5 mile (800m). Opposite the confluence of the Ribble and the Hodder, go over a stile by a bench.

> ### WHAT TO LOOK OUT FOR
> One plant to look out for, especially along the riversides, is butterbur. This is another name that will ring bells with Tolkien devotees; there's an innkeeper in The Lord of the Rings called Barliman Butterbur. The flower spikes, which appear in early spring, look superficially like dull pinkish hyacinths, but the individual flowers are daisy-like. Later in the year huge leaves develop, these were traditionally used to wrap butter.

4 The narrow path quickly rejoins the track. At Winkley Hall Farm go left to the houses, right between barns then left past a pond and out into a lane. This climbs steeply then levels out, swinging left past Winkley Hall. Go through a kissing gate on the right and across the field to another. Keep straight on across a large field, just left of a wood, then down via stile and up to reach a road.

5 Turn right down a pavement to the river. Immediately before the bridge, turn left along a track. Follow the river round, climb up past Hodder Place then descend again to a bridge over a stream.

> ### WHILE YOU'RE THERE
> Stonyhurst College was originally the home of the Shireburn family and much of the original Elizabethan house still exists, though almost enveloped by vast 19th-century additions. It was taken over in 1794 by Jesuits fleeing the French Revolution and is now a leading Catholic boarding school. It's open to visitors during the summer holidays.

6 Go up the track on the left, cross a footbridge and then climb a long flight of wooden steps. Follow the top edge of a plantation then cross a stile into a field. Keep to its edge and at the end cross a stile into a stony track. Keep left, past Woodfields and out to the road. Go down the track by the post-box to Hall Barn Farm and along the right side of the buildings.

7 Turn right and walk along a tarmac track for 200yds (183m). Go left through a gate by the end of a wall and along a narrow field. Drop down to the right on a track alongside a wood then up to a kissing gate. Follow the field-edge to another kissing gate. At the top of the final field, through a gate, a narrow path leads to a short lane. At its end turn left back to the start of the walk.

> ### WHERE TO EAT AND DRINK
> In the absence of a Green Dragon or Prancing Pony, The Shireburn has the most Tolkeinesque name, and it's a very comfortable place, if a little bit upmarket for hobbits. (You'll probably want to change out of muddy boots first.) There's a smart restaurant as well as a good range of bar food.

Over Birdy Brow

An extension taking in woodlands, a fine viewpoint and a secret dell.

See map and information panel for Walk 38

DISTANCE 8 miles (12.9km)	**MINIMUM TIME** 2hrs 45min
ASCENT/GRADIENT 804ft (245m) ▲▲▲	**LEVEL OF DIFFICULTY** ✦✦✦

SUGGESTED MAP OS Explorers 287 West Pennine Moors; OL41 Forest of Bowland & Ribblesdale

WALK 39 DIRECTIONS
(Walk 38 option)

From the small bridge at Point ❻, climb the wooden steps parallel to the river then take the footpath on the right to a stone cross. Beyond this the lower path turns out easier, after the initial scramble down over tree roots. The paths rejoin as the slope eases.

On emerging from the wood at a footbridge, turn left and head straight up the hill to a stile on the skyline 200yds (183m) left Rydding's Farm. Go left on the track for 400yds (366m) then go left across the field to a power line pole. Go up left to a gate and out into the road (known as Birdy Brow). Climb it steeply then, just below the zig-zag (Point ❹), go left along a track.

Follow the drive in front of the first house and then back left. Cross two stiles left of Lowfield Cottage. From the corner of the farm, bear right up the hill just right of trees that appear, to a stile. Slant right across the field corner. Over the fence in the next field is the ancient Paulinus or Kemple End Cross.

Follow the fence, then a wall, to the left. From the next stile descend towards the right side of Fell Side Farm. Go over two stiles then straight down, left of Fell Side Barn. Keep straight on, joining a track in a dip alongside a stream. Follow the track to the road by a cottage (Point ❸).

Go right 70yds (64m) then go left on the track to Higher Deer House. Go through a gate at the end, slightly left to another, then across the field to a stile above the wooded valley of Dean Brook. Descend to a footbridge (Point ❿) then bear left, zig-zagging back right half-way up. At the top keep right to a stile in the corner then follow a narrow path to a track. Just above is Greengore, used as a hunting lodge in the 16th and 17th centuries.

Go left 150yds (137m) then left again on a narrower path. Follow this down to a bridge and continue down the main track above the Dean Brook. Where the track forks take the lower one. About 200yds (183m) beyond some cottages take the narrow path on the right to another tarmac lane and go left, emerging almost opposite the Bayley Arms. Turn right back to the village hall.

Clitheroe's River and Castle

Partly a town trail, but mostly a rural walk beside the River Ribble.

DISTANCE 3.5 miles (5.7km) **MINIMUM TIME** 1hr 30min

ASCENT/GRADIENT 164ft (50m) ▲▲▲ **LEVEL OF DIFFICULTY** +++

PATHS Field paths, surfaced tracks, pavement, 7 stiles

LANDSCAPE Urban, rural, woodland and riverside – a rare mix!

SUGGESTED MAP OS Explorer OL41 Forest of Bowland & Ribblesdale

START / FINISH Grid reference: SD 743422

DOG FRIENDLINESS On lead around livestock and on streets

PARKING Long stay pay car park on Chester Avenue, by Clitheroe Station

PUBLIC TOILETS On Church Walk

WALK 40 DIRECTIONS

From the car park walk towards the railway then bear right on a road blocked to traffic. Follow it round to Kirkmoor Road and go right. At Back Commons go through a kissing gate. Cross the field to another, bear right to a third kissing gate and, immediately right through one more. Go right past the cemetery to the road and go left for 250yds (229m).

Go right, up the lane then, just past the gates of Park Hill, go left on a footpath. Cross the field to the edge of the wood. Go down left then swing right on a surfaced track. Follow this for

WHERE TO EAT AND DRINK

The Swan and Royal Hotel, on Castle Street has well-kept Jennings ales and a good range of bar food – try the baguettes with a variety of fillings to choose from– as well as a children's menu. The Exchange Coffee Company, on Wellgate, also does lunches and delicious cakes.

WHAT TO LOOK OUT FOR

Clitheroe is built on limestone, which is visible at Cross Hill Quarry, in the riverbed and in the knoll on which the castle stands. Many of the town's buildings are of limestone too, but darker gritstone also appears, quarried a short distance away (there are still active quarries on Waddington Fell, for instance). When you walk down Kirkmoor Road, the terraced houses on one side are built of gritstone while those opposite are built of limestone.

150yds (137m) then descend steps to river level near the boundary of Cross Hill Nature Reserve.

The reserve centres on Cross Hill Quarry, which ceased working in the 1900s. Like others in the area it once served the cement industry (which is still active, as you'll see). The woods near the river produce masses of wood anemones by early March: these star-like white flowers are among the earliest signs of spring. From below the quarry fork left and along the river bank for about

0.75 mile (1.2km) upstream to Bradford Bridge, near the huge cement works, incongruous in the pastoral Ribble Valley.

Cross the bridge and, from the bend in the road, go left to follow the river bank through the first field, then go diagonally right to a gate. Keep left where other paths branch off, then via a stile cross a larger field to a concrete footbridge. Bear left across the next field, near the river, then join a track up and right past Brungerley Farm to the road.

Go left across Brungerley Bridge. Go over the wall by the bus shelter and down the steps. Follow the river bank to a gate into Boy Bank Wood. Ignore an obvious line of steps on the left and follow a level, though rougher, path to the large weir opposite Waddow Hall. On the far side is a fish ladder, and on our side an old sluice gate. The canal, now partly silted up, ran for about 0.5 mile (800m) to the large mill at Low Moor, formerly owned by the Garnett family of Waddow Hall.

Beyond the sluice the steep bank on the left begins to diminish. Go up and back left along the top of the bank, to meet a clear path (coming up from the steps you passed earlier). Turn sharp right across the field to the end of a line of trees and a kissing gate. Follow the left edge of the next field. At the next gate you briefly rejoin the outward route, going slightly right to a gate and across the last field to Back Commons.

Keep straight on down Kirkmoor Road, swing right and out to a busier road. Cross the railway bridge. From the end of its parapet double back to the right, under the little footbridge that serves the Methodist chapel.

Enter the castle grounds and turn left immediately up a rising road. Approaching the top but before the parapet, go left on a broad and level path above the bandstand. Follow this round below the castle walls to the main entrance.

The Castle Museum has recently reopened after a major restoration project, with new interactive displays and improved access. Mind you, it's still quite a puff to the very top, but the breathtaking views of the town and wider valley are well worth the effort.

From the main entrance walk out along Castle Street. The distinctive wedge-shaped building at the end of the street is now the town library, but in its time it has also been town hall, police station, lock-up, and public lavatories! The area in front of it was the original market-place, but it's a very cramped site. Markets used to overflow into Castle Street and Church Street.

An arch beside the White Lion leads into Church Walk. Go left at the bottom, then right, to the railway station. The main building is now a gallery, but the railway is still busy, with trains to Manchester. Go right 50yds (46m) and under the tracks to return to the car park.

WHILE YOU'RE THERE

The Castle Museum seems larger on the inside than it does on the outside, and is good on geology as well as history. Don't miss the Geological Trail at Salthill Quarry on the outskirts of the town. Clitheroe has good shopping too – lovers of sausages and/or wine will be in seventh heaven.

Breezy Brine Fields
of Knott End

*An easy walk exploring an unexpected and curiously salty corner
of Lancashire's coastal plain.*

DISTANCE 5.5 miles (8.8km)   **MINIMUM TIME** 1hr 45min

ASCENT/GRADIENT 115ft (35m) ▲▲▲   **LEVEL OF DIFFICULTY** +++

PATHS Quiet streets and lanes, farm tracks and sea wall, 3 stiles

LANDSCAPE Short built-up section, seashore, farmland and golf course

SUGGESTED MAP OS Explorer 296 Lancaster, Morecambe & Fleetwood

START / FINISH Grid reference: SD 347485

DOG FRIENDLINESS Can run free on sea wall, under close control elsewhere

PARKING Free car park by end of B5270 at Knott End

PUBLIC TOILETS At side of coastguard building adjacent to car park

---

The salt industry in this part of Lancashire is not of the same antiquity as that in Cheshire and has not had the same profound impact on the landscape, but it still played a significant part in shaping the present scene.

Rock Salt

Extensive deposits of rock salt lie below the surface around Knott End and Preesall. In the early days of the industry, natural brine was found but more commonly it is extracted by pumping fresh water down bore holes to dissolve the rock salt. The first such wells in this area were drilled in the 1890s and many of the well-heads can still be seen, often standing incongruously in the middle of fields surrounded by contentedly grazing Friesians.

Chemical Foundations

The brine fields provided the raw material on which the ICI Hillhouse chemical plant, just across the Wyre, was founded, producing chlorine as well as salt. This has developed subsequently to produce a much wider range of chemical products.

There's no feel of an industrial town about Knott End today, which is a mixture of modest resort and commuter village. At low tide the sands are exposed for miles, far out into Morecambe Bay, and when it's clear the Lakeland skyline makes a wonderful backdrop.

Pilling Pig

As you leave the built-up area, you meet the trackbed of the railway line that once linked Knott End to the main line at Garstang. The line was affectionately known as 'The Pilling Pig', a name derived from the note of the whistle of an early engine. The section to Pilling was opened in 1870 but the extension to Knott End had to wait until 1908. It closed in 1963.

When you leave the old trackbed you climb a small rise – almost the only one you'll encounter on the whole walk – and from the far side, beyond Curwens Hill, you get your first sighting of the brine fields. To begin with they may look like nothing more than farmland, but then you'll notice several pools – the walk soon passes close by one – left by subsidence.

Creeks and Salt Marsh

As the walk continues, you'll see more and more reminders of the salt industry, especially along the track from the lane out to the sea wall. You follow this northward, with extensive creeks and salt marsh off to the left, and views across the Wyre to the chemical works and to Fleetwood.

Flying golf balls add spice to the next part of the walk. There's an interlude as you pass Hackensall Hall. The present building was erected in 1656 by the Fleetwood family, but later passed into the hands of the Bournes and was extensively renovated in the 19th century. There's more golf course to cross before returning to the sea wall for the last stretch.

WALK 41 DIRECTIONS

❶ Go out to the sea wall, turn right past the ferry, along the road past the Bourne Arms and then along the Esplanade. Where the main road swings away, keep on along the seafront, down a private road then a short stretch of footpath. Where this ends, before a grassy stretch of seafront, go right down a short side-street then straight across the main road into Hackensall Road. Go down this almost to its end.

WHAT TO LOOK OUT FOR

The well heads, pools, and one small extraction plant all bear witness to the salt industry. The fields provide good grazing for dairy cattle and also for a large number of brown hares. They are larger than rabbits, with longer legs and ears. They don't burrow but rear their young in shallow scrapes in the ground.

❷ Just before the last house on the left take a public footpath which, beyond woodland, becomes a straight track. Follow this through a thin belt of trees, across fields and then beside a wooded slope. Where the wood ends go through an iron kissing gate on the right then up the edge of the wood and over a stile into the farmyard of Curwens Hill farm. Keep ahead through this and down a stony track, which swings left between pools. It becomes a surfaced lane past some cottages.

WHERE TO EAT AND DRINK

There's a café adjacent to the car park and a couple of others in the village. The Bourne Arms is close by; a large pub with a conservatory at the back, and generous portions of pub food.

❸ Join a wider road (Back Lane) and go right. It becomes narrow again. Follow this lane for about a mile (1.6km), over a slight rise and down again, to Corcas Farm.

❹ Turn right on Corcas Lane, signed 'Private Road Bridle Path Only'. Follow it through the brine fields. After 0.5 mile (800m) it swings left by a caravan site.

❺ Go right, past a Wyre Way sign and over a stile on to the embankment. Follow its winding course for about a mile (1.6km) to a stile with a signpost beyond.

❻ Keep ahead on a clear tractor track under power lines. When it meets the golf course, the track first follows its left side then angles across – heed the danger signs! Follow the track to the right of Hackensall Hall. Just past its main gates go left on a track with a Wyre Way sign. This skirts round behind the outlying buildings.

❼ The path swings to the right and then crosses the golf course again. Aim for a green shelter on the skyline then bear right along the edge of the course. Skirt round some white cottages, then go left to the sea wall. Turn right along it, to return to the car park.

WHILE YOU'RE THERE

For most of the year, a small passenger ferry regularly makes the short crossing to Fleetwood. The town was planned as an integrated whole in the 1830s and 40s by the architect Decimus Burton, at the instigation of Sir Peter Hesketh-Fleetwood from nearby Rossall Estate. The Fleetwood Museum tells much more about the salt industry. Britain's oldest surviving tram system links Fleetwood with Blackpool.

The Bottom and the Top: Around Beacon Fell

A very popular slice of upland Lancashire countryside, by turns both expansive and intimate.

DISTANCE 6 miles (9.7km) **MINIMUM TIME** 2hrs

ASCENT/GRADIENT 689ft (210m) ▲▲▲ **LEVEL OF DIFFICULTY** +++

PATHS Field paths, in places indistinct, clear tracks, 19 stiles

LANDSCAPE Forest, heathland, farmland, woodland, riverside

SUGGESTED MAP OS Explorer OL41 Forest of Bowland & Ribblesdale

START / FINISH Grid reference: SD 565426

DOG FRIENDLINESS Dogs should be under close control throughout

PARKING By Beacon Fell visitor centre

PUBLIC TOILETS At visitor centre

With a name like Beacon Fell, expect a prominent hill. An outlier of the Bowland Fells, its altitude of 873ft (266m) may seem comparatively modest but its detached position gives excellent sight lines – and it was much more accessible for those who had to man the beacon!

Part of a Network

In the days before telegraph and telephone, beacons were the nearest thing to instantaneous communication. Admittedly they couldn't convey any detail, but they did serve to warn of great events. Most famously, a network of hundreds of beacons – of which this was one – spread the news of the appearance of the Spanish Armada in 1588.

From this history, and some contemporary publicity, you might reasonably expect 360 degree views, but at the present time stands of conifers block out the southern half of the panorama. However, you get much of the 'missing' half anyway, early in the walk, as you descend the southern flank of the hill. Preston figures prominently. Alongside the anonymous tower blocks are the Preston North End football stadium at Deepdale and the slender spire of St Walburge's Roman Catholic Church, the tallest church spire in Britain after Salisbury Cathedral.

Brock Bottom

You wend your way across farmland, pleasantly enough, and then drop abruptly into the enclosed valley of the River Brock, usually referred to as Brock Bottom. A paper mill existed here in 1786, but was replaced soon after by a larger cotton mill. The mill site is just downstream when you reach the river, while on the way upstream you'll see remains of the millstream, dam and sluices. Since the mill closed in 1923, the valley has been popular with Preston folk. In the days when a bicycle was the most likely means of transport it was a handy distance from the town.

From the bridge at Brock Mill (don't be confused; this is not the main mill site previously referred to) you climb again. Rougher pastures, ill-drained and with large stands of rushes, intervene before the steeper climb through forest on to the upper slopes of Beacon Fell. Here there are large open areas, now being managed as heathland.

The summit view may expand with forest clearance in years to come but even now the half that you can see is grand. Mostly it's a fairly local prospect, over Bleasedale to the higher Bowland Fells. These rise to 1,673ft (510m) at Fair Snape Fell, but the most prominent is the abrupt end of Parlick. When the wind is right you'll usually see hang-gliders here (there's a gliding club below) as well as an enticing slice of the Lakeland skyline.

WALK 42 DIRECTIONS

❶ Look for a public footpath sign in the left-hand corner of the lower car park by the visitor centre. Go down the broad, shady track, then through a field. Bear left towards Crombleholme Fold

and walk through the farmyard. Turn right on to a lane to a bend.

❷ Go left, cross a stream then up a track swinging right. After 50yds (46m) go left, slanting gently down to a stile just before the field ends. Make for a gate at the far end of the field then angle right to reach a low bridge and up the track beyond.

3 Go through the Cross Keys car park, through a farmyard and into a field. Go right to a stile then straight on to the corner of a hedge. Follow it to a tree then angle left to a stile. Go right then straight ahead to a lane and go left.

WHILE YOU'RE THERE

Longridge is a modest town with a few specialist shops. A little further away, on the banks of the River Ribble, is Ribchester. This is one of the most important Roman sites in Lancashire, with a nicely-presented museum. The White Bull Inn, at the stone-built heart of the village, has pillars which probably originated in a Roman bath house.

4 Go right to Lower Trotter Hill. Cross a cattle grid, go left, then round to the right and past a house. Go through the left-hand gate and up to a stile. Follow the field-edge, eventually bending left. Go down a stony track and then turn right on a road.

5 As the road bends to the right keep walking straight ahead. Descend on a sunken track through woods and cross a footbridge. Go up a few paces, then right, and follow obvious

WHERE TO EAT AND DRINK

About 3 miles (4.8km) south of Beacon Fell is the village of Goosnargh, where the Grapes Inn, next to the parish church, serves meals all day and often does themed food nights on weekday evenings. There's a good selection of real ale and the pub even has its own bowling green.

WHAT TO LOOK OUT FOR

There are three main classes of 'grass-like' plant. True grasses have round, hollow stems (bamboo is a grass). Sedges have solid stems with a triangular section. They are mostly found in damp or infertile soils – many of the 'grasses' on the moors are actually sedges. Finally, rushes have round solid stems. The soft rush is a common example. It grows in damp places but its clumps usually provide a sound footing.

paths near the river to reach Brock Mill picnic area.

6 Cross the bridge then go through a gateway on the left. Bear right up a track then go right, through rhododendrons. Follow the edge of a wood, then go right, crossing the stream. Go up a field-edge and straight on towards Lower Lickhurst. Go round into the drive and up to the road. Go left for just a few paces, then go right, up a drive. Keep straight on as it bends left, up fields to a lane. Go right for 140yds (128m).

7 Go left over a stile and diagonally to an isolated thorn tree. Continue almost level to a gateway and then to a stile and footbridge. Follow an old boundary, now a muddy depression, then bear left to power lines. Follow these to a marker post. Go right, directly uphill. Cross the road to a track rising through forest. At a junction go left for 200m (183m) then right up a narrow path to the summit trig point.

8 Bear right along the edge of the forest then left across a boardwalk. Keep ahead to return directly to the visitor centre.

Overleaf: Beacon Fell, Lancashire (Walk 42)

WALK 43

The Picturesque
Crook O'Lune

A well-loved local beauty spot, but beauty isn't just skin-deep.

DISTANCE 3.25 miles (5.3km)   **MINIMUM TIME** 1hr 15min

ASCENT/GRADIENT 164ft (50m)   ▲▲▲   **LEVEL OF DIFFICULTY** +++

PATHS Tracks, pavement, woodland and field paths, 5 stiles

LANDSCAPE Great river bend, steep woods and open valley

SUGGESTED MAP OS Explorer OL41 Forest of Bowland & Ribblesdale

START / FINISH Grid reference: SD 522647

DOG FRIENDLINESS Care needed on cycleway and road, can run free elsewhere

PARKING At Crook O'Lune, just off A683

PUBLIC TOILETS At car park

L andscapes change; rivers change their courses, for instance, although at Crook O'Lune, the river has followed much the same route since the last ice age. It's what geographers call an incised meander, where the river has cut down into solid rock. Further upstream, the valley floor is composed of clay, sand and gravel and the river can shift course much more easily. You get a great view of the Crook from the first bridge. Looking upstream, the hill peeping over the trees is Clougha Pike (see Walk 46).

You leave the river to visit Gray's Seat, named for Thomas Gray. Best known as a poet, Gray was also a leader of the Picturesque movement. In the 18th century fashionable gentlefolk began to travel widely. Some of the first guidebooks instructed them precisely where to observe the best views and how to judge them. As the name 'Picturesque' suggests, the real landscape was judged largely on its fitness to make a picture. Gray visited here in 1769. Here's a sample of his pronouncement:

'…in the richest of vallies, the Lune serpentizes for many a mile, and comes forth ample and clear, through a well-wooded and richly-pastured foreground. Every feature which constitutes a perfect landscape of the extensive sort is here not only boldly marked but also in its best position'

You can form an impression of the view Gray saw, but much has changed. Half a century later, the great artist J M W Turner also visited; his painting shows a far less wooded foreground (and no caravan site).

After completing the swing round Crook O'Lune, you break out into the wider valley above. Lush riverside pastures give easy walking, with the distinctive outline of Ingleborough forming the background. You cross the river on a waterworks bridge, built in 1881, carrying water from the Lake District to Manchester. Looking upstream, you can see that the river 'serpentizes'. Older maps show how the river has changed its course. (Walk 44 covers this ground).

WALK 43

CROOK O'LUNE

Lancaster

A683

Gray's
Seat ③

④

②

⑤

①

⑥ Caton

Escowbeck Beck

Artle Beck

Dismantled Railway

60

40

A683

0 ½ mile
0 500m

Halton
Park ●
Hawkshead

100

A

140

Lower
Highfield

159

Waterworks
Bridge ⑦

Over Lune
Barn ●

Aughton
Woods

Middle
Highfield ●
B

Far
Highfield ●

River Lune

Aughton
Barns ●
C

Aughton

163

N

A683

WALK 43 DIRECTIONS

❶ From the corner of the car park go down shallow steps to the old railway line. Turn right, under the road, along a short shady track, then cross a bridge high above the river. Go down steps to the right then double back under the bridge you've just crossed.

❷ Follow a well-trodden path close to the river bank until a steep path with occasional steps leads up to the right. At the top there's a signpost. Go right to a gate, cross the busy road with care, and then continue right for 150yds (137m) to a gap in a stone wall on the left. There's a sign for Gray's Seat. Follow the enclosed path, with a few rocky steps, to Gray's Seat.

❸ Return down the enclosed path to the road, back along the pavement, and cross again, back to the signpost and through the gate.

❹ Go right, initially level and almost parallel to the road but soon descending, with more steps, back towards the river. The path levels out and then forks. Swing left through a fine grove of beech trees, and over a small footbridge and a stile as you leave the woods. Follow the path along the river bank. Cross a small side stream, Escow Beck, by a footbridge and follow the curving river bank past picnic tables. Go up to a kissing gate, cross over the road, and then go through a gate almost directly opposite to you.

❺ Bear left down towards the river, over a footbridge, then round to the right under the old railway bridge. It's easy going now, following the river bank upstream for over 0.75 mile (1.2km) to Artle Beck. This is crossed by an arched footbridge.

❻ Continue up the river bank for 440yds (402m) to the waterworks bridge. Go round to a stile at the far side of the small building, through a kissing gate and up the steps. Cross the catwalk.

❼ At the end of the bridge drop down left. (A diversion into the first wood is worth the effort, especially in the bluebell season.) Follow the river bank briefly then bear right to a bridge. Keep on the level across the next field to a stile at its far end. Go over this into another wood and follow a clear path through it. All that remains is to follow the river bank back to the bridges and the car park.

High Fields and River Banks

A longer walk which climbs above the valley for a much wider view.

See map and information panel for Walk 43

DISTANCE *8.25 miles (13.3km)*   **MINIMUM TIME** *3hrs*

ASCENT/GRADIENT *590ft (180m)* ▲▲▲   **LEVEL OF DIFFICULTY** ✦✦✦

WALK 44 DIRECTIONS
(Walk 43 option)

After crossing the road at Point ❺, keep ahead to the cycleway and go back across the river to the car park. From its end by the 'artist's easel' go left through a gate. Follow the path to the road and turn right for 200yds (183m).

Turn right and follow a lane past Halton Park (Point **Ⓐ**). Continue for 275yds (251m) then go right up the track to Hawkshead farm. Just before the first barn go left. Skirt the farm, pass a marker post, and cross a stile by a tree on the skyline. Go left along the hedge then keep straight ahead and through a wood.

Descend to a stream then go up to Lower Highfield. Beyond a gate follow the waymarks left around the edge of the hilltop field. Continue, by a high stone wall, to Middle Highfield (Point **Ⓑ**).

Go over the stile, turn left, then right on a cobbled path between buildings. Keep straight on, between more houses, then follow a tall hedge over the highest of the high fields. There are extensive views, especially of the wind turbines across the valley.

Aim right of Far Highfield, to reach a stile. Descend rightwards

to a footbridge. From another stile slant down to a stile alongside a gate, overlooking Aughton. Bear left, above the line of trees, to the road. Descend into the village and straight across the 'crossroads'.

Aughton is the home of the largest pudding in the world. Every 21 years, since 1824 and probably earlier, the villagers produce a colossal plum pudding – the 1992 version weighed 5,000lb (2,270kg). All because a boiler, used to soften willow wands for basket making, resembled 'a gert puddin boiler'.

The lane descends steeply then a track continues, past Aughton Barns (Point **Ⓒ**), towards the River Lune. Veer away from the river bank at a small marker post, towards a distant gate. Follow the slightly higher ground – the former river bank – to Over Lune Barn. Follow the river bank round the rest of the great bend until it swings sharply back left. Where the river meets the steep wooded slope, go up to a stile and some steps. A narrow but clear path runs through Aughton Woods. At the far end, the waterworks bridge is seen just ahead. Go through the 'tunnel' and rejoin Walk 43 at Point ❼.

Glasson and Cockersand

A very easy walk, at its most atmospheric on a blustery day.

DISTANCE 5.5 miles (8.8km)   **MINIMUM TIME** 1hr 45min

ASCENT/GRADIENT 82ft (25m) ▲▲▲   **LEVEL OF DIFFICULTY** ✦✦✦

PATHS Village streets, tow path, lanes, tracks and sea wall, 11 stiles

LANDSCAPE Level fields, a wide estuary and rocky foreshore

SUGGESTED MAP OS Explorer 296 Lancaster, Morecambe & Fleetwood

START Grid reference: SD 446560

DOG FRIENDLINESS Grazing land, dogs need to be under close control

PARKING Car park at East Quay, Glasson

PUBLIC TOILETS Across road from car park

WALK 45 DIRECTIONS

From the car park, turn left to walk along the edge of the harbour and then continue walking up the canal, past the church to Brows Bridge.

It's immediately apparent that Glasson Dock is a working port, albeit on a modest scale, as well as being home to many pleasure craft. Lancaster itself, about 5 miles (8km) up the Lune, suffered a sharp decline in trade in the early 19th century. The opening of the canal link to the sea at Glasson, in 1826, only partly stemmed the drop in the area's fortunes. Glasson is now a minor outpost of the Port of Lancaster, which centres on the deep-water harbour at Heysham.

Unfortunately, the Lancaster Canal never achieved its full economic potential because it was not linked to the rest of the national network of canals. Ironically this has now changed with the building of the Millennium Ribble Link in 2002.

Go up to the bridge and cross it. After 100yds (91m) fork left into Jeremy Lane. Just after a sharp double bend there's a footpath sign on the right over a culvert and over a stile. Follow the right field-edge, round to the left and over a stile, over another culvert bridge and along an obvious track.

Go left at a junction along the lane to Kendal Hill farm. Just after the bungalow, but before the farm itself, cross a stile on the right, then another beside a drinking trough. Walk down past the farm to another culvert and continue straight ahead for about 0.5 mile (800m) over various footbridges and stiles. From a substantial bridge over a ditch, go straight ahead to a gap then along the side of the field towards Crook Cottage. The track alongside leads to the sea wall.

Go left, and then left again by Lighthouse Cottage, then turn right at the next junction. At the second sharp left-hand bend there's a gate on the right with a smaller gate alongside. Follow the

WHERE TO EAT AND DRINK
In addition to cafés and pubs in the village there's the highly regarded The Stork at Conder Green. You can walk there, along the old railway line, a return trip of about a mile (1.6km). There's well-kept ale and a good selection of food served in hefty-sized, walker portions.

track to the right of the farm, and out to the picturesque ruins of Cockersand Abbey.

The site is most evocative on a wild day, but even then it's hard to imagine how isolated it must have been in the 12th century, when Hugh Garth, 'a hermit of great perfection', came here. It was then a virtual island. Erosion has pushed the shoreline closer while the marshes, which then stretched several miles inland, have now been drained — you've just walked across them. The site was relatively safe from marauders and well-removed from worldly temptation. It subsequently became a hospital and then a Premonstratensian priory. The only standing building is based on the Chapter House. A few other fragments of masonry remain.

WHILE YOU'RE THERE
Glasson itself is worth a little more time: there's usually something going on in the outer harbour or the inner yacht basin. There's also a gallery/craft shop and, at the back of the Dalton Arms, the Smokehouse offers a wide range of delicacies.

From the ruins, walk out to the sea wall. If the tide's not too high it is worth venturing on to the foreshore, where you may find great drifts of mussel and cockle shells. These shellfish are still harvested commercially in Morecambe Bay.

About 0.25 mile (400m) out, at the mouth of the Lune channel, is a small lighthouse. This still works, for the benefit of those craft which use the Lune channel. These are relatively few and it's much more probable that you'll see container ships or the Isle of Man ferry heading to or from Heysham, beyond the low spit of Sunderland Point. The harbour itself is just beyond the obvious and unsightly nuclear power stations.

Turn right along the sea wall, which brings you back to the junction by Lighthouse Cottage. Retrace the short section to Crook Cottage but continue to Crook Farm. Turn right just before the houses and along a track. After a gate on a bridge it becomes little more than tractor ruts as it swings towards a line of hawthorns, then becomes clearer again. Continue to walk alongside a caravan site, then a lane leads out to a road. Go left on the road and up to Tithebarn Hill.

There's no sign of a tithe barn today, but this is the highest point of the walk at 60ft (18m). The view indicator isn't as easy to read as it once was but it's clear enough. And isn't it good to know that Coniston Old Man, in the Lake District, is just 27.75 miles (44.6km) away (especially if you can't see it)?

Directly opposite, at the mouth of the river, is Sunderland. The road to the village still floods at high tides. Turn right down Tithe Barn Hill, walk into the village and across the swing bridge or lock gates. The car park's just beyond, on the right.

Down to the Summit on Clougha Pike

A wild walk to a deceptive 'summit', which proves an unrivalled viewpoint overlooking the sweeping Bowland Fells.

DISTANCE 5.25 miles (8.4km)	**MINIMUM TIME** 2hrs
ASCENT/GRADIENT 1,050ft (320m) ▲▲▲	**LEVEL OF DIFFICULTY** +++
PATHS Mostly very rough moorland, often rocky, 4 stiles	
LANDSCAPE Moorland with some rocky outcrops, above green valley	
SUGGESTED MAP OS Explorer OL41 Forest of Bowland & Ribblesdale	
START / FINISH Grid reference: SD 526604	
DOG FRIENDLINESS Access Area – dogs not permitted	
PARKING Access Area car park at Birk Bank	
PUBLIC TOILETS Nearest at Crook O'Lune (see Walk 43)	

Clougha Pike is the finest viewpoint in the Bowland Fells, possibly in the whole of Lancashire. There's lots to see at closer quarters too and the walk is always rewarding, but on a clear day it's nothing short of magnificent. Although the ground is sometimes very rough, the ascent is rarely very steep and the views expand with every stride.

The Ridge of Clougha

The opening stages are almost level. After crossing the little aqueduct called Ottergear Bridge, the route swings round and climbs a little, then drops into a small, sharp-cut valley. This is the first of several curious channels, some of which cut right through the ridge of Clougha. These are relics from the end of the ice age. The edge of the ice sheet was stationary for a while in this area, dammed up behind the ridge. Torrents of meltwater pouring off the ice, and probably sometimes running underneath it, carved the network of channels. The most striking example is Windy Clough, seen near the end of the walk.

Heather Moorland

Now the walk begins its steady ascent across the broad flanks. Apart from a few wet patches marked by rushes and cotton grass, the dominant vegetation is heather and bilberry. Heather moorland is widespread in Britain but rare in most of the rest of Europe. Geology, climate and soils are partly responsible, but the management of the land is equally significant. Controlled burning of areas of moor encourages the heather to produce new shoots, the main food for the red grouse. Like it or not, grouse shooting for sport is part of the ecology of these moors.

When the rocky crest of the ridge is reached, the climbing is over. The last stretch is generally level and when the summit of Clougha appears it definitely is slightly below you. This hardly detracts from the view, even though a sector is blocked by the higher ground of Grit Fell and beyond it Ward's Stone, the highest summit in Lancashire.

CLOUGHA PIKE

Distant Views

The Clwydian Hills in Wales are apparent much more often than the higher, but more distant, peaks of Snowdonia. The distinctive profile of the Isle of Man, over 60 miles (97km) away in the Irish Sea, is also visible on a clear day. However, what grabs most of the attention is the sweep of the Lakeland skyline and the continuation of high ground eastwards, over the Howgill Fells and into Yorkshire, where the Three Peaks of Whernside, Ingleborough and Pen-y-ghent are dominant.

As you descend, the nick of Little Windy Clough appears over your right shoulder, and then the much deeper Windy Clough appears. The stream draining Windy Clough runs underground where we cross it but surfaces again a little lower down.

WALK 46 DIRECTIONS

❶ Follow the track above the car park, then fork left. It becomes a green path, running generally level, to Ottergear Bridge.

❷ Turn left and walk along a level track, then bear right at the next junction. The track climbs slightly, descends into a narrow valley, then climbs steeply up the far side before it finally eases and swings round to the right.

❸ Go left on a narrow path, running almost level above a steeper slope. After 500yds

(457m), it angles back down into the valley. Follow the base of the steep slope and cross a small stream. After 30yds (27m) a green track climbs to the right.

❹ Wind up steeply to near-level moor. The path follows a slight groove, then skirts leftward around a boggy patch parallel to the wall. The grassy path ahead is initially very faint. Keep just left of the continuous heather and it soon becomes clearer. There's another grooved section then a clear stony path rises leftward across steeper ground.

❺ As the slope eases the path remains clear, passing a few sketchy cairns. Follow a groove, past tumbledown shooting butts. As the ground levels, ease right past cairns and marker stakes to an ugly new track. Cross and follow a thin grassy path with more marker stakes. Bear right up a slight rise and join a wider path at a cairn. Go right on a broad ridge, crossing a fence, to reach the summit trig point.

❻ Descend a clear path on the right past a large cairn. There's a steep drop nearby on the left, with some small crags. A fence converges from the right, eventually meeting a wall.

❼ Scramble down rocks by the end of the wall. Continue down its left side for about 300yds (274m). Bear left at a levelling amid scattered boulders. Descend through a gap flanked by wrinkled rocks then across gentler slopes to a gate by the corner of a wall.

❽ Head straight down until the ground steepens, then swing right and weave down towards Windy Clough. From a stile go left down a grooved path to an area of young trees. Fork left, closer to the stream, rejoining wetter alternative routes above larger oaks. Descend through gorse then follow duckboards skirting a bog. Turn right along a track then left over a slight rise to the car park.

Leck Beck and Ease Gill Kirk

A brief glimpse of the subterranean mysteries of limestone and a lot of fine wild country.

DISTANCE 7.5 miles (12.1km)   MINIMUM TIME 3hrs

ASCENT/GRADIENT 968ft (295m) ▲▲▲   LEVEL OF DIFFICULTY +++

PATHS Field paths, indefinite moorland paths, quiet road, 5 stiles

LANDSCAPE Sheltered river valley, wild moorland, gorge and pot-holes

SUGGESTED MAP OS Explorer OL2 Yorkshire Dales – Southern & Western

START / FINISH Grid reference: SD 643767

DOG FRIENDLINESS Under Access Land restrictions, dogs must be on a lead and keep to the rights of way (no dogs permitted in Access Area)

PARKING Park by Leck church (honesty box)

PUBLIC TOILETS Nearest at Kirkby Lonsdale, 2 miles (3.2km) up A65

Yes, this is still Lancashire. A long wedge of countryside squeezed between Cumbria and North Yorkshire, with the highest ground in the county along the borders, reaching 2,251ft (686m) on Crag Hill. But it hardly feels like Lancashire: the landscape, with its limestone gorges, scars and pot-holes, is what you expect of the Yorkshire Dales.

High Drama

The crucial thing about limestone is that it dissolves in water far more readily than other rocks. It can produce gentle beauty, as around Silverdale (see Walk 48), or it can yield high drama, as it does here. First, however, there's a lengthy preamble, following Leck Beck from green pastures to open moors, where you're as likely to see hen harriers as other walkers. The drama begins with the gorge of Ease Gill Kirk. You can enter both its upper and lower reaches, though a vertical rock step blocks the direct connection between the two. The lower section of the gorge is particularly impressive, with leaning rock walls punctured by several cave entrances.

Limestone Caves and Gaping Holes

Most of these are gloomy passages, which many people will find uninviting if not actually repellent, though you can see evidence of digging undertaken by cavers to enlarge the entrances. At the back, just to the right of the rock step, is another cave, which you can safely look into. Some extra light enters from a slot high on the left.

It's back into the open on the wide moors above Ease Gill Kirk. Initially there are only faint sheep tracks to follow, but you soon pick up an old wall and then a path. But the drama's not over, as the level moor is pockmarked with holes, from shallow pits to gaping shafts. Fortunately all the dangerous ones are fenced off. The most blatant is Rumbling Hole. It gets its name from the constant sound – actually more of a tapping – of water striking stones at the bottom, 360ft (110m) down. Short Drop Cave is less spectacular, with a narrow entrance where the stream can normally be heard not far below.

LECK BECK

Lost John's Cave, near the road, is the most important to cavers because of the extent of its underground passages. Further down, where the road runs in a slight valley, there's a small entrance right by the road, normally covered and bridged by scaffolding poles from where intrepid cavers start their descent into the gloomy cave interior.

Even if you normally hate road walking, the finish of this walk should win you over. The grass verges are kind to your feet and you'll often go the whole way without meeting a single car. Wide views stretch over Morecambe Bay and the Lake District at first, but as you lose height the perspective changes and increasingly it's a Lune Valley view.

WALK 47 DIRECTIONS

1 Turn right on the road then right again. Turn left by a post-box and go down a lane, bearing right at the bottom.

2 At the end of the tarmac take the lower, left track to a stile then continue on a good tractor track. Just after crossing a stream the track divides. Go left through a gate into a wood then through a long pasture, passing a small wooden house. Cross a stile at the far end into 'open access' country. The track descends almost to river level then climbs away again.

LECK BECK

3 Climb fairly steeply for about 300yds (274m) then go left in a slight dip past the ruins of Anneside. The path, now little more than a sheep track, runs fairly level and fairly straight until it meets a ruined wall. Cross the dip of a small stream then bear left out of it, crossing damp ground on to a grassy shoulder. Follow the crest of steeper slopes dropping towards the beck to arrive at the brink of a tree-filled gorge.

4 Go straight ahead on a narrow path across the slope. It's not difficult, but it's clearly no place to slip. This leads into the upper reaches of Ease Gill Kirk. Look around, then retrace to the crossroads and descend to a more level area below some small outcrops. Cross a steep grass slope into the gorge. After exploring return to the crossroads.

WHERE TO EAT AND DRINK

There are no facilities at Leck. You can get tea, coffee and sandwiches at Cowan Bridge Village Stores but for meals and alcohol go straight across the A65 and 2 miles (3.2km) down a narrow lane to The Highwayman at Nether Burrow, on the A683. There's plenty of room indoors and out.

5 Now head directly south-east uphill (not the track above the gorge) taking a sharp right on the faintest of paths through the bracken and heather to reach a ruined wall. Follow this up to the left then along, above some rocky outcrops to a green conical pit. Keep trending uphill and to the right, on sheep tracks, to meet a long, straight, dry-stone wall. Follow this until several fenced holes appear in a shallow dip on the left. Bear left to the nearest one, then follow a narrow

WHILE YOU'RE THERE

Kirkby Lonsdale, just up the A65, is an old stone-built market town full of nooks and crannies. It has been widely used for film and TV locations. It's best known for its church, parts of which are Norman, and for Ruskin's View, just beyond the churchyard. Just outside the town is Devil's Bridge, an elegant medieval structure, below which are limestone outcrops and deep pools in the Lune.

footpath past the second and third. Follow a shallow valley with no permanent stream to the deep, fenced shaft, which is known as Rumbling Hole.

6 Turn right on a faint footpath across level moorland to another fenced hole, about 200yds (183m) away, called Short Drop Cave. From this cave head back towards the dry-stone wall and, just before reaching it, head up to the left to join the road. Turn right to walk down it. After 150yds (137m) Lost John's Cave can be seen away to your left.

7 Continue walking down the quiet road for another 2.5 miles (4km) back to Leck. Finally turn left near the church to return to the start of the walk.

WHAT TO LOOK OUT FOR

Along the way you will see some large-scale features like caves and gorges, which are one result of limestone wearing away in water, but it also produces distinctive features on a smaller scale. Many outcrops are marked by runnels and flutings, and level surfaces often form expanses of limestone pavement. These may appear flat from a distance, but the action of rain water often produces deep cracks.

A Quart in a Pint Pot: Around Silverdale

An easy-going walk, yet fascinating with its continuous changes of scenery.

WALK 48

DISTANCE 5.5 miles (8.8km)   MINIMUM TIME 2hrs

ASCENT/GRADIENT 426ft (130m) ▲▲▲   LEVEL OF DIFFICULTY +++

PATHS *Little bit of everything, 9 stiles*

LANDSCAPE *Pot-pourri of woodland, pasture, village lanes and shoreline*

SUGGESTED MAP *OS Explorer OL7 The English Lakes (SE)*

START / FINISH *Grid reference: SD 472759*

DOG FRIENDLINESS *Can run free on shore and in woods*

PARKING *Small National Trust car park for Eaves Wood*

PUBLIC TOILETS *In Silverdale village*

The Arnside–Silverdale Area of Outstanding Natural Beauty (AONB) is barely longer than its name, yet intricate and exquisite. Unfortunately – for this book, anyway – half of it is in Cumbria. This walk attempts the impossible, to sample all of its delights in one go.

A Mosaic of Habitats

The AONB covers a mere 29 square miles (75sq km) yet includes rocky coastline, salt marsh, wetland, pasture, woodland, heathland, crags and quarries, and some attractive villages, principally Silverdale in Lancashire and Arnside in Cumbria. With such a mosaic of habitats, it's no surprise that the area is rich in wildlife – more than half of all British flowering plant species are found here.

There's a fine start, through Eaves Wood with its yew trees and impressive beech ring, then the route sidles through the back lanes of Silverdale before reaching the coast. The channels of Morecambe Bay shift over time and so does the shoreline. The band of salt marsh around the Cove has shrunk drastically in the last few years. At high tide the rocky foreshore may be impassable, in which case follow an alternative footpath across open fields of The Lots safely above the shore.

By the Sea

The route avoids a tricky section of the coast south of Silverdale, returning to the shore near Jenny Brown's Point. The breakwater running out to sea recalls a failed 19th-century land reclamation scheme. Just around the corner stands the tall chimney of a copper smelting mill that operated around 200 years ago.

After Heald Brow comes Woodwell, the first of three springs on the walk. At Woodwell the water issues from the crag above the square pool. This was used for watering cattle but now you're more likely to see dragonflies. Woodwell and the other 'wells' around Silverdale are found where the water-permeable limestone is interrupted by a band of impermeable material such as clay. Rainfall generally sinks quickly into

SILVERDALE

limestone and there are no surface streams over most of the area, so the springs were of vital importance. This rapid drainage also means that few of the footpaths are persistently muddy, even after heavy rain.

Lambert's Meadow, however, is usually damp. It sits in a hollow where fine wind-blown silt (known as loess) accumulated after the last ice age. The soil is dark and acidic, very different from that formed on the limestone, and the plant community is different too.

WALK 48 DIRECTIONS

1 From the end of the National Trust car park at Eaves Wood, follow the footpath to reach a T-junction. Go right a few paces and then turn left, climbing gently. Keep left to the beech ring, then straight on. Just beyond a junction veer left to a wall and continue walking on this line to reach a lane.

2 Cross on to a track signed 'Cove Road'. Keep ahead down a narrow path (Wallings Lane), a drive, another track and then another narrow path to a wider road. After 200yds (183m) go left down Cove Road.

3 From the Cove walk leftward, below the cliffs, to the shore. Walk up the road to Beach Garage then take the footpath alongside. (If high tide makes this route impassable follow the easy footpath across the fields above.)

4 At the next road turn right for 600yds (549m) then bear right down Gibraltar Lane for 350yds (320m). Enter the National Trust property of Jack Scout.

5 Descend left to the lime kiln then follow a narrowing path directly away from it. This swings left above a steep drop and descends. Follow a broad green path to a gate. After 150yds (137m), another gate leads into the lane. At its end continue below Brown's Houses along the edge of the salt marsh to a stile. Go up slightly, then along to a signpost.

6 Turn left, climbing steeply to a gate. The gradient eases, over rock and through a lightly wooded area into the open. Go left to a stile then follow a wall down and into a small wood. Follow a track down right. Cross the road to a gap

in the wall, descend, then walk below the crags to Woodwell.

7 The path signed 'The Green via cliff path' leads to a rocky staircase. At the top go ahead to join a broader path. Follow it left, slant right, then continue into woodland. A stile on the right and a narrow section lead to a road. Go right 150yds (137m), then left into The Green. Keep right at a junction then join a wider road.

8 Go left for 75yds (69m) then right, signposted 'Burton Well Lambert's Meadow'. The track soon descends then swings left, passing Burton Well on the right. Cross a stile into Lambert's Meadow, then go right, over a footbridge to a gate. Climb up, with some steps, and continue more easily to a fork. Go left alongside a pool (Bank Well) into a lane. Go left and at the end the car park is virtually opposite.

To Leighton Moss

A gallon in a quart pot — the diversity of Arnside–Silverdale in one shot.

See map and information panel for Walk 48

DISTANCE 8.75 miles (14.1km) **MINIMUM TIME** 3hrs
ASCENT/GRADIENT 837ft (255m) ▲▲▲ **LEVEL OF DIFFICULTY** ✦✦✦

WALK 49 DIRECTIONS
(Walk 48 option)

At the signpost (Point **6**) go right to follow the embankment. Cross the sluice at the end then go left under the railway and out to the road (Point **A**). Fields on the right are being restored to wetland. Turn right along the road for 300yds (274m) and then left up Crag Road.

After 600yds (549m) there's a track on the left. Follow it for 0.5 mile (800m) to a gate on the right, past an interpretation board for Warton Crag. A green path rises gently through open woodland, then another gate leads into thicker woods. The trees obscure any obvious sign of the Iron Age hill-fort that once existed here.

Go straight on at a signpost, past the beacon, until the view opens out above Warton Crag (Point **B**). The magnificent panorama extends from the Bowland Fells, over Morecambe Bay, to the Lakeland skyline.

Return to the signpost and bear right. After 400yds (366m) fork right by a split boulder and descend a rock cutting into a tree-filled bowl. Fork left as the gradient eases then descend again in a shallow trough. At the bottom, near a wall, go left. The path roughly follows the wall then meets a stony track. Descend this to the road.

Go left, straight up for 700yds (640m), then swinging right. About 250yds (229m) past the gates of Leighton Hall there is a footpath on the left that has been made wheelchair-accessible. Follow it to reach Summerhouse Hill (Point **C**), overlooking Leighton Hall.

Descend to the curve of the drive by the hall then fork right into a walled lane. Follow this for 0.5 mile (800m) to Grisedale Farm. Roughly 100yds (91m) further on, fork right and join the causeway across Leighton Moss. Half-way along is the public hide (Point **D**).

At the end go right on the road for 150yds (137m) then cross to a gate. Cross the golf course on a public footpath to a belt of woodland. Cross the track to a path winding through the overgrown former Trowbarrow Quarry. Cross the track again by an information board, go down a path and cross the railway. From the white gate go right to a lane. Go left, then right. At the next junction go left on Park Road back to the car park.

Time-honoured
Lancaster

A castle, historic waterfront and attractive streets in Lancashire's finest town.

DISTANCE 3 miles (4.8km) **MINIMUM TIME** 1hr

ASCENT/GRADIENT 262ft (80m) ▲▲▲ **LEVEL OF DIFFICULTY** +++

PATHS City streets, paths with setts, canal tow path

LANDSCAPE Basically urban, but with good leavening of open space

SUGGESTED MAP OS Explorer 296 Lancaster, Morecambe & Fleetwood

START / FINISH Grid reference: SD 474619

DOG FRIENDLINESS Can run free on tow path, care needed on busy roads

PARKING Parksafe at Mitre House, northbound on one-way system

PUBLIC TOILETS At car park and in city centre

WALK 50 DIRECTIONS

Exit the car park to a cobbled haven beside a busy road. In front is Covell Cross and above it the 17th-century Judge's Lodgings, which houses a furniture museum and a museum of childhood. Go up, with the Judge's Lodgings on your right, on to Castle Hill.

Shakespeare's phrase 'Time-honoured Lancaster' originally described not a city but a man, John O'Gaunt, 2nd Duke of Lancaster. The imposing gateway known as John O'Gaunt's Gate was built during the reign of his son, Henry IV. Walk up to its left, then round behind the castle to the visitor entrance.

Large parts of the castle are still in use as a prison, while the remainder also houses lawcourts. When these are not in session tours take in the courtrooms, the ancient dungeons, the magnificent Shire Hall and the Drop Room, where the condemned awaited execution – among them the Pendle Witches (see Walk 33).

Go through the gateway into the Priory churchyard. (A short detour rightwards gives a fine view over the city.) The church is among the finest in Lancashire, one of its most notable features being the superb 14th-century choir stalls. From the west front of the church, walk down a narrow path (known as Vicarage Lane). Half-way down a sign points right to the slightly disappointing Roman bath house remains.

Return to Vicarage Lane, descend steps, cross a cycleway/footpath and continue down the last bit of Vicarage Lane to St George's Quay. Turn left and walk about 300yds (274m) to the Maritime

WHILE YOU'RE THERE

You can't miss the Ashton Memorial, crowning the ridge east of the city. (It's equally conspicuous, and often puzzling, to travellers on the M6.) Variously called 'the Taj Mahal of the North' and 'England's grandest folly', it was built between 1906 and 1908.

LANCASTER

Museum. This old building was originally the Customs House (1764) during the brief period when Lancaster was a major port.

Return along the riverside towards the Millennium Bridge. Walk up the ramp on to the bridge, go right, then bear left along the old railway line. Reaching the main road, slope off right and through the underpass. Emerging on to the open grassy Green Ayre, bear left and walk up beside the river to admire Skerton Bridge. Completed in 1788, the bridge is notable as the first bridge in England with a level roadway.

Turn around then bear left past the skate-board park towards the traffic-lights. Cross the street on your left, turn right and cross again when lights permit. Go up steps into a car park. Leave by the vehicle exit then cross the road above and go up Alfred Street almost opposite. Turn left into De Vitre Street, second right into Shaw Street and then through a gap at its end.

Turn right along the canal tow path. Several cotton mills still stand, though they now serve other functions. Go under two bridges and below the grand Roman Catholic Cathedral, designed by the Lancaster firm of Paley and Austin.

At the third bridge the tow path changes sides, by a spiral ramp that allowed horses to cross without being unhitched. Continue past the White Cross pub. The White Cross complex originally produced oilcloth but now houses a wide variety of educational, office and light industrial activities. Continue under another bridge then cross by the footbridge just before the Water Witch.

Cross the road into Queen Street – another collection of good Georgian houses – and down to Queen Square. Bear left along the main road for 100yds (91m) to a pedestrian crossing, then turn right down Common Garden Street. At Marks and Spencer turn left into pedestrianised Penny Street. At Horseshoe Corner, turn left up Market Street to Market Square. The City Museum here was formerly the town hall, built in 1781 and replaced by a much more grandiose but less beautiful one (off the walk route) in 1909. There are some very good displays upstairs that tell much more about the history of the area.

Continue past New Street then look for a narrow entry (Music Room Passage, also called Sun Street) on the right, which leads into Music Room Square, named for the enigmatic building at the back. Follow Sun Street to its end and turn left up Church Street. The pedestrian crossing at the top returns you to Covell Cross.

Walking in Safety

All these walks are suitable for any reasonably fit person, but less experienced walkers should try the easier walks first. Route finding is usually straightforward, but you will find that an Ordnance Survey map is a useful addition to the route maps and descriptions.

RISKS

Although each walk here has been researched with a view to minimising the risks to the walkers who follow its route, no walk in the countryside can be considered to be completely free from risk. Walking in the outdoors will always require a degree of common sense and judgement to ensure that it is as safe as possible.

- Be particularly careful on cliff paths and in upland terrain, where the consequences of a slip can be very serious.

- Remember to check tidal conditions before walking on the seashore.

- Some sections of route are by, or cross, busy roads. Take care and remember traffic is a danger even on minor country lanes.

- Be careful around farmyard machinery and livestock, especially if you have children with you.

- Be aware of the consequences of changes in the weather and check the forecast before you set out. Carry spare clothing and a torch if you are walking in the winter months. Remember the weather can change very quickly at any time of the year, and in moorland and heathland areas, mist and fog can make route finding much harder. Don't set out in these conditions unless you are confident of your navigation skills in poor visibility. In summer remember to take account of the heat and sun; wear a hat and carry spare water.

- On walks away from centres of population you should carry a whistle and survival bag. If you do have an accident requiring the emergency services, make a note of your position as accurately as possible and dial 999.

COUNTRYSIDE CODE

- Be safe, plan ahead and follow any signs.

- Leave gates and property as you find them.

- Protect plants and animals and take your litter home.

- Keep dogs under close control.

- Consider other people.

For more information visit www.countrysideaccess.gov.uk/things_to_know/countryside_code